Doing My Duty

Doug "Curly" Anderson
82nd AB Division
Europe : WWII

Doing My Duty

The Life Story of Douglas "Curly" Dickerson

by

Doug Dickerson

as told to Bruce Washburn

SECOND EDITION

Celo Valley Books
Burnsville, North Carolina

> Copies of this book may be obtained by sending (for each copy) $14.00 + $2.50 for shipping and handling. Send your request to:
> Doug Dickerson
> 2200 Cornwallis Drive, #219
> Greensboro, North Carolina 27408

Doing My Duty

The Life Story of Douglas "Curly" Dickerson

By Doug Dickerson
As told to Bruce Washburn of Goose Wings Passages,
Greensboro, North Carolina
Book and cover design by Michael and Michelle Crouch

Second Edition
November 1998

ISBN 0-923687-50-5
Library of Congress Catalog Card Number 98-88342
Copyright © 1998 by Douglas Dickerson
All rights reserved.
Printed in the United States of America

No part of this book may be reproduced or transmitted in any form or by any means, electronic or mechanical, including photocopying, recording, or by any information storage and retrieval system, without permission in writing from the publisher, except short excerpts used in reviews, in which full publishing information is given.

*Dedicated to my late wife,
Edna Lee Kearns Dickerson,
and to the men that shared
these experiences with me.*

Contents

Foreword ix

Chapter One   Growing up   1

Chapter Two   Playing ball   19

Chapter Three   Joining a new team   41

Chapter Four   Fighting in Sicily   59

Chapter Five   Fighting in Italy   71

Chapter Six   Regrouping in England   77

Chapter Seven   Fighting in France   81

Chapter Eight   Fighting from Holland to Germany   89

Chapter Nine   Coming home and going on   97

Chapter Ten   Honoring those who did their duty   119

Addenda

My Brothers   131
Medals, badges, commendations   139

Foreword

On the night of June 5, 1944, just hours before the invasion of Normandy officially began, I found myself on the top of an outhouse in France. My third nighttime combat parachute jump had landed me on that ridiculous and perilous perch. Not the sort of place you want to be if the stuff starts hitting the fan.

But, it could have been worse.

I was no stranger to outhouses or bullets, having had unforgettable experiences with both when I was a small child growing up dirt poor in the South.

I was only two years old the first time I was shot. That happened in our home in Greenville, South Carolina. I was sitting on the floor, chewing an old rag doll as my mother was kneeling near me, cleaning out an old trunk.

We didn't have much, but we did have the pistol that Mother's grandfather had used during the Civil War, and that was kept in the trunk. Mother laid it out and continued her cleaning as my brother Herman, who was 6, picked up the pistol unnoticed. He pointed it at me, told me to "stick 'em up," pulled the trigger — and the gun fired!

The bullet entered my right hand, the one I was holding the doll with. It could have hit me in the throat or the head, too, but the powder was so weak that the bullet just lodged in my hand. A doctor removed the slug, but to this day, 76 years later, I still have the scar.

When I was 3, I got diphtheria and almost died. But I survived that, as well as all the other childhood diseases, plus a second bout with diphtheria when I was 5. I had to learn how to walk again after the second go round with diphtheria.

In between my bouts with diphtheria, my parents — Raymond Rufus Dickerson and Blanche Eva Welker Dickerson — moved me and my three brothers — Fred, Herman, and Glenn — to Reidsville, North Carolina.

It was in Reidsville that I had my first experience with using an outhouse as a landing zone.

We were living on Main Street and across the street a little ways up was a vacant lot. There had been an old house there, but it had been torn down and moved. One afternoon about 5 o'clock, we were out playing cops and robbers and I was running across that vacant lot when I suddenly found myself falling. When the property owner had torn down the old house, he hadn't filled up the hole where the two-seater outhouse had been!

It must have been four or five feet deep and I just disappeared into it. I went down in it up to my chest, and I had that stuff all over me. It took my mother an hour to clean me off. She took buckets of water — we didn't have a hose — and kept pouring and pouring and pouring until she got it all off me.

I can't say that I came out of that experience smelling like a rose, but I wasn't hurt. I guess I've always been lucky.

The sun was shining as it rose in the East when I was born on the morning of March 5, 1920. I've had my share of growing pains, like all people, good and bad. I've thrived on being a good person and Jesus has had his hand on my shoulder many times.

I have been fortunate to survive mankind's worst war, and to be able to share some of my skills with youngsters as a teacher and coach and father.

Now, at age 78, I want to share my story with others in the hope that it will help them know a bit about what I and many other American men went through as we came of age in this tumultuous time called the 20th Century.

As the sun is setting for me in the West, I hope that I have served my community, my state, and my country well. I feel blessed to have lived the life I've lived.

Douglas "Curly" Dickerson
1998

*This is my favorite photograph of myself.
It was taken in Ireland in 1943.*

Chapter One — Growing up

I was always lucky, but I had one brother who wasn't. His name was Clayton and I didn't even know about him being my brother until I was 4 or 5 years old. Clayton was born two years before me. My oldest brother, Fred — who is 9 years older than I am — remembers Clayton and what happened to him.

Fred told me that he and my other brothers — Herman, Glenn, and Clayton — were playing in the backyard when the three oldest boys decided to go in the house, leaving Clayton in the small fenced-in yard by himself. A short while later, Mother asked Fred to go out and check on Clayton. When Fred didn't see him in the yard, he went to the small woodshed in the back and saw Clayton draped over the edge of a large bucket there.

Fred picked him up and could see mucus running from his nose and felt that his body was limp. He yelled, "Clayton's dead!" and Mother, who had just come out to the woodshed, screamed. Fred told me that he doesn't remember what happened after that, except that a doctor came and confirmed that Clayton had drowned. The bucket had just enough water so that it had covered his nose when he had tipped over in it, apparently while swishing a cap in the water. Clayton couldn't get his feet back under himself after he fell.

I don't know how my father reacted to Clayton's death, but he was one of those men who didn't seem to be able to ever get a solid footing for himself either. He was sort of a drifter. He really wasn't trained to do anything in particular. He worked some in the coal mines up in West Virginia, and worked in a cigarette factory for the American Tobacco Company in Reidsville,

He also worked with handmade cigars. He was very good at mixing tobaccos for handmade cigars, and my mother worked at that, too. They made the cigars in bunches and got paid according to how many bunches of 25 or 50 they made. They got paid 25 cents a bunch and were lucky to make about a dollar a day. They did that in Reidsville and in Greensboro in the late '20s and '30s.

My father did a lot of carpenter work, too. Right before he died, he was doing a lot of housepainting. He had to be kind of a jack-of-all trades because he didn't go beyond the first grade in school, and my mother went to about the second grade. That's about all the schooling they had.

He was from Greensboro, North Carolina, originally and my mother was from the Rudd community out at Browns Summit, outside Greensboro. My daddy was born in 1890 and my mother was born in 1894. I don't know how they met.

My dad was tall and skinny. He must have been about 6'2" or so, and real thin. My mother was a small woman, not much over 5 feet tall and about 95 pounds. A little bitty woman, but they used to call her "Dynamite." This friend of mine, Pinky Riddick — he was about the same size she was — he called her that. She was right spunky, and she worked all her life. She had to.

When she was 10 years old, she went to work at Proximity Mills in Greensboro. Had to stand on a box to operate the machines, and got 10 cents an hour at nighttime.

Her momma was Ida Clayton Welker. Her daddy — Theodore Welker — had a little farm, but carpentry was his main job, and farming was more or less a sideline. He helped build all the mill houses in the Proximity, White Oak, and Revolution communities in Greensboro. He had an old mule he would ride to work from the Rudd community.

My mother had one sister and two brothers, and she was the oldest child. Lawrence was the second. He became a proofreader or teletype operator for the Roanoke Times in Virginia. Hunter, the other brother, became a carpenter and contractor. Grace was the youngest child and she eventually operated a little antique store in Luland, Texas. My mother didn't talk much about her childhood.

She was the one who did everything around our house, and everything that could be done for us boys. She had to work and take care of the house and cook.

Fred was her first child. Mother was 16 years old when he was born in 1911. She had another child — all boys — about every two years after that, with me being the last. Glenn was born in 1913, then came Herman, Clayton, and me in 1920. I think my mother was pregnant with me when Clayton drowned.

I didn't grow up with my father much because he wasn't around too much. When he was, we would catch baseball and he always treated me real nice. My mother said he never spanked me, so I guess we got along pretty good, but in those days, you didn't associate much with your father, other than baseball. That was a big thing with him. I think he played a little semi-pro ball, but with who, I couldn't tell you. We used to catch baseball a lot though when he was home.

I saw my dad administer discipline one time. We were living in Reidsville, close to Lawsonville School. I was about 6 years old when he caught Herman smoking. Back then, most men shaved with a straight razor and had leather razor strops to sharpen their blades. My dad had half of one cut in five strips, which he kept in the shed, and I saw him spank Herman with that on his bare bottom. Herman didn't sit down for a week. I don't think it did much good for Herman, but I remembered that!

That was the only time I ever saw him beat any of the boys or switch or spank them. I learned my discipline right there.

My daddy was not a religious man. I don't remember either him or my mother ever going to church, but all of us boys went to the Presbyterian Church. I think my parents were a little bit embarrassed to go because we had nothing. We were just as poor as you could be when it came to clothes and things like that. I think that's one of the things that may have stopped them from going, but I don't know that. But, we were brought up in the church as kids and we weren't as loud and boisterous as other kids. Didn't cut-up and carry-on. We followed the rules of discipline.

My father never did say much, but my mother used to say, "Always treat people nice.

It's much easier to be nice than it is to be bad." She was, more or less, our mentor.

I don't know what my parents were doing in Greenville, South Carolina, before we left there in 1924. We were all together — all four of us boys — when we moved to Reidsville, but we were separated a lot as kids and didn't grow up as a close family because we were on our own so much and had to move so much. Many a time we just didn't have any money to pay the rent and food was scarce — a lot of times we didn't have much to eat at night. I can count 14 times that we moved before I got out of high school. Moving around so much like we did, you know there was bound to be something wrong.

My dad was a heavy smoker when he was with us and he did drink, but not around us. And I think that he ran around, too. My mother never told me that, but in later years she told my wife, and my wife told me.

Anyway, the first place we lived in Reidsville was in the country, a farm off highway 87, going towards Burlington. It was about a mile or two from Reidsville. My first memory about that place is when I was 4 or 5 and was in the yard, looking up at three hogs hanging from what looked like a goal post. It was hog-killing time and they had scalded them. Those hogs looked like they were all hung to heaven to me, so big and stretched out. And there was a big ole black kettle where they made soap and stuff, and it was out there that day, and they were throwing meat in there — rabbits, squirrels, hog meat, vegetables — to make a Brunswick stew for everyone to eat.

There was a creek behind our house there

and I would take my inner tube down there and splash around in the water. One day, all three brothers — Fred, Glenn, and Herman — came and got me out of the creek, along with two neighbor boys who had a big pond by their house. They took me up to that pond and threw me in and I couldn't swim. I was screaming and squealing, but I dog-paddled out of it, and there's where I learned to swim. I was 5.

After a while, we moved into Reidsville and there was a swimming pool back off Main Street where they would let us little fellows go in for free. People there got a big kick out of throwing pennies in the pool and watching us dive for them. By the time I was 8, I got so I could swim the whole length of that thing and back underwater.

When I entered the first grade in Reidsville I went to Lawsonville School and that was about the time I began having regular chores to do. I'd come home from school and I'd get in the kindling and coal and do little things like that. Momma was working at the American Tobacco Company and would get home about the time school let out. One day I came home and wanted to play before doing my chores. Our community was mostly a colored town and if Momma wasn't home, I'd play with a little colored boy named Billy who lived next door. We were about the same age. I wanted to play that day and I started backtalking my mother when she told me to do the chores first. I was being sassy and real smart.

My brothers heard me and, man, they swooped down on me, picked me up, took me out to the shed, and beat my butt. Pulled my britches down and spanked me, saying, "Don't you ever do that again. You say, 'yes ma'am, no ma'am, yes sir, and no sir!'" All three of them spanked me and said, "Buddy, you'll get it again if you do that again!" I remember that to this day and I still say, "yes sir, no sir, yes ma'am, and no ma'am!" I learned real quick...not that my grades showed it in school, however.

My first grade teacher at Lawsonville School was Miss Stanley. I remember one day at school at lunchtime, it had snowed a little bit and it was icy, and they let us go out and play. There was a walkway going from the front of the school down towards the street and I was sliding on the ice on it when I fell and bumped my head real hard and got a bad headache that lasted all day.

I remember that Miss Stanley held me in her lap the rest of the day. Back then they wouldn't send you home because most people worked and they didn't have telephones, so they couldn't call anyway. It stands out in my mind that she let me sit in her lap most all of the day and then let me go home when school was over.

Another thing I remember about the first grade. They used to do a little play about a rabbit and a tar baby. I was playing the tar baby in that skit and was standing up against the wall on the little stage, which was slanted, while we were practicing one day. I had to go to the toilet so bad, but I didn't know what to do, and I was scared to ask the teacher...and I started pissing in my pants. It ran down my leg, all the way down the stage, and I was embarrassed to death. The only good thing about it was that it was late in the afternoon, so I just went on home in wet pants.

I went to a school on Franklin Street in

Reidsville in the second and third grades, and the only time I got in trouble when I was in school was when I was in the third grade there. I don't know why I did it — I think someone else was doing it, too — but I had a little mirror and the sun was shining in the window, and I kept reflecting it into the teacher's eyes. She made me go out and get a switch and she switched me right there in front of the class.

There was another time that same teacher had to attend to me, too, but that was because of an accident. There was a house near the school ground with a fence around it. It was a wire fence on one side and a plank fence on the other and there was a telephone pole right at the end where they came together. They had a bunch of chickens there and they'd lay their eggs right along the fence. I picked up one of those eggs one day — I reached through the wire fence — and I threw it at the telephone pole which was some 10 or 12 yards away. And about that time, a boy came around the corner of that plank fence and I hit him right between the eyes. And that egg was rotten!

I'm telling you, that stunk so bad that I can remember it to this day. The teacher made me take him to the toilet and clean him up. I wasn't even throwing at him, either. He just came around that corner at the wrong time.

I was always good at throwing. One of our games as kids was playing "Annie Over." We'd use a tennis ball or a rubber ball and one kid would be on one side of the house and another kid would be on the other side. You'd throw the ball over the house and see if the other fellow could catch it. You didn't know where it was going to come over and you would get a point if you caught it. We'd play to a score of 10 or 12.

We played marbles a lot, too, and jacks, and hide-and-seek. I used to love shooting marbles. A lot of times you'd play with marbles in a circle and try to shoot them out. Other times you'd dig holes and you'd shoot around the holes.

When we played baseball, our ball would be made out of a rubber ball wrapped with string and with tape around that. We'd buy a bat for a quarter and both teams would use it. If it broke, somebody would take it home and fix it — tape it up and bring it back.

We didn't have any organized ball teams in elementary school or junior high back then. Didn't really have any organized sports until you got into high school. We could play a little baseball during recess at school, but we didn't have long to play then.

We'd play ball when we weren't in school though, and there was a family there in Reidsville — the Sacrinty family — that owned a soda shop, and they were always so good to all the kids because they all loved sports. Their soda shop was across the street from where my mother and father worked in the cigar factory.

The Sacrinty family had three boys — Bo, Nick, and John — that I played ball with, and their girl, Avra, was in my third grade class. We'd all play ball together then we'd go into the soda shop and instead of drinking a Coke or something, we'd drink carbonated water straight out of the bottle. It burned! Anyhow, their mother and daddy loved not only their own kids, but they loved us, too. I went to see them frequently until my family moved again in 1929 when I was 9.

First we moved to Burlington, North Carolina for a few months, then moved again that same year to Greensboro. When we moved to Greensboro, our family kind of broke up, and I didn't see my brothers much anymore. Fred stayed out with my grandparents in Rudd, and Herman stayed in Reidsville at the Sanitary Cafe on Scales Street, right in the middle of town. The high school coach there kept him because he was such a good football player and so for two years, he lived upstairs over the cafe and worked down there on the weekends. He got fed and had a place to live. Hap Perry was the coach who watched over him. Herman was about 14, somewhere along in there.

Meantime, Glenn and I were with our parents. Glenn's health wasn't real good and, as a child, I noticed he had a bad cough at times. Later, as a young man, he learned he had tuberculosis and spent a number of years in a sanitarium.

In Greensboro, we first lived with relatives in a big gray house, the only two-story house on West Northwood Street. There were only six houses on the whole block, even though we were in the city limits. The house belonged to my dad's sister, Pearl Dickerson Permar. When we moved in there I slept on a cot in a walk-in closet.

After moving to Greensboro, we didn't go to the Presbyterian Church anymore. There was a little church right across the street from my Aunt Pearl's house — a little Baptist church that my grandfather on my daddy's side built. He built Pearl's house and that church. We'd had outhouses where we'd lived before, but at Aunt Pearl's we had an indoor toilet!

Pearl had a bunch of kids and she played the piano in that church, and her daughter, Elizabeth, played the piano, too. I would walk over there with them on Sundays. Her kids were Elizabeth, Norma, Edgar, Catherine, Marie, and Ann. Norma was about my age and I was between her and Edgar in age.

I didn't know my daddy's dad or anything about him. My brothers didn't know anything about my daddy's family either. My daddy had a brother whose wife, Maude Dickerson, lived over in Proximity and ran a boarding house, but I didn't know him either.

While we were living with Aunt Pearl, I began trapping rabbits in the nearby woods to help feed the family and earn a little money. I made rabbit gums — box-like traps several feet long with a trap door. My daddy helped me make those and I would go out and check them each morning. I made double gums, too, and one morning I caught two rabbits at one time. I was afraid to take the rabbits out of the traps, so I would get my daddy to take them out.

Later, me and a good friend, Aubrey Apple, would run rabbits. He had five good rabbit dogs, and we'd take the dogs — wouldn't use a gun — and we'd run with the dogs the best we could. Of course, we couldn't keep up with them, but we'd hear them barking and follow them. They'd run the rabbits down and we'd get them. We got 13 one day.

We'd skin them and the family would keep so much and I'd sell the remaining rabbits for 15 cents apiece up at Hobbs' Grocery Store, where Anton's Restaurant is now.

We'd also go to a little nearby creek and catch "knotty-heads," little fish with knots all over their heads. We'd use a regular straight pin and bend it, make a cork, put a little bitty weight on the line, and just get a stick and that was our fishing pole. We'd use worms for bait.

While we were staying with Aunt Pearl, I went to Irving Park School for the 4th grade. We had a teacher there, Miss Andrews, who was sort of tomboy-like and she'd play softball with us every day. She had a dress on, but she was good!

I don't remember too many other teachers from my elementary school years. I attended Aycock School in the 5th and 6th grades. However, my family continued to move and we lived on several different streets including Wendover and Smith. By the time I was 11 or 12, we were living on Dillard Street near McIver School.

That was when I got my first job, delivering milk at 2 o'clock in the morning when I was 12 years old. I'd get up at 1:45 in the morning and a man — I don't remember his name — would come by with a horse and buggy and pick me up. We worked for Rock Creek Dairy and they would send the milk in to what was called the Bishop Block, up on North Elm Street. It's demolished now, but it was up from the Presbyterian Church, on the left-hand side. We'd go down there and get the milk and deliver it from 2 to 5 o'clock in the morning for 10 cents an hour.

My job was to take the milk and put it on the front porch. He'd take one side of the street and I'd take the other. I'd deliver milk or eggs or whatever they wanted, three times a week: Tuesdays, Thursdays, and Saturdays. And every Saturday, they would give me a quart of milk and a dozen eggs. I didn't have any milk as a child until I started getting it from the dairy then. That wasn't part of my pay, they just gave me that on Saturdays. I'd take it home and we'd all eat it, me, Mom and Dad. Glenn was no longer living with us then. He had finished high school at Greensboro High and had gone to Lees-McRae Jr. College in Banner Elk, North Carolina.

During this time, I was also selling the Grit newspaper. I was making a penny a paper selling it house-to-house in the afternoons. It was published once a month. I was also selling Cloverine Salve, which a lot of people sold. It came 12 to a tube and I'd get a nickel for each one I sold. They were 25 cents each. I was selling in the neighborhood around Dillard Street and McIver School. I'd also pick up bottles and got a penny for each of them.

I had never had a bicycle, so when I worked for the dairy and sold papers, I began saving up to buy a good Seminole bicycle for $11. I finally got $6 and went to Masters bicycle shop on Gaston Street downtown. I put $6 down and had to pay a dollar a week. Each week, I toted milk and sold papers and I'd go down to that shop and pay my dollar. And after I had paid that last dollar five weeks later, I got my bicycle and I had money left to go to the show. So, I rode it up to the National Theater, which was four blocks away. There was a chain on the bank building beside the theater and I locked my bicycle to that chain and went to the show — and when I came back it was gone!

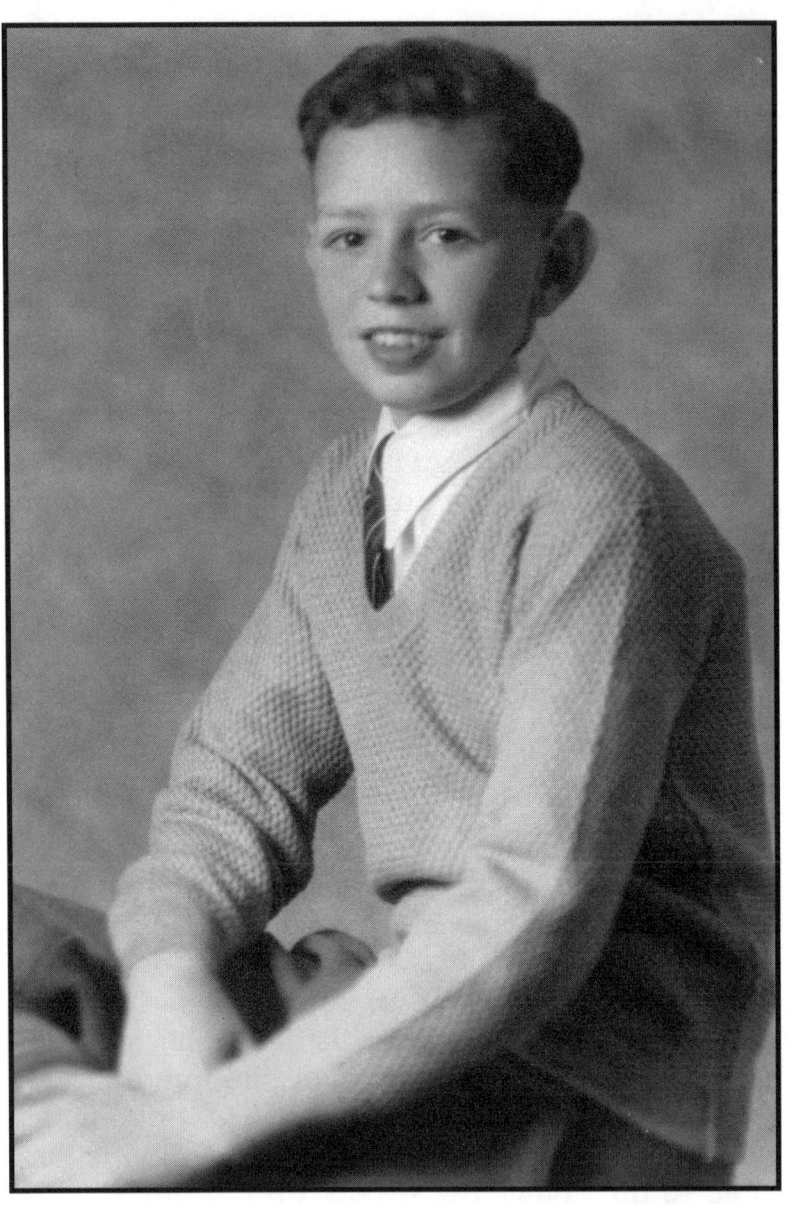

*I was 12 years old when this was taken.
I was delivering milk and selling Grit and Cloverine
Salve door-to-door and feeling prosperous.*

It had been stolen.

That bicycle was the only thing I had had in my life — I didn't have skates even. I was 12 years old and I cried. My dad and I went to the police and reported it, but we never did get it back. Losing that bike hurt me more than anything else ever had. There wasn't much my daddy could say.

It was going to the show that also led to me getting my nickname. You could go to the show for 10 cents, so I'd get 20 cents, and four or five of us boys would go to the show together on Saturdays at the National Theater on South Elm Street. After the movie, we'd go by Jim's Lunch. It was on the corner from the theater, close to the railroad tracks, and we'd get a Pepsi and hotdog for a nickel each, and then we'd go around the corner to McMaster's Service Station on the corner of McGee and Greene. They had funny papers — "Curly and the Kids" — that they would give us for free, and that's where I got my nickname, because I had curly hair, too.

Everybody called me Curly — the teachers, coaches — everybody but my parents. They called me Douglas. Nobody in that neighborhood knew my first name but my parents, I think.

I began to get interested in football and baseball when I was 12. I had played some ball in sandlots before then, but not much. In the summer, we'd go up to McIver School on W. Lee Street and choose up sides every morning about 10 o'clock. Of course, I, being the youngest, went out to right field, and I batted last.

Around this time I got involved in organized baseball. The Rotary, Civitan, and Elks clubs had organized baseball teams for the little fellows — around the ages of 11, 12, and 13. Those were the only organized teams I remember for kids. Of course, our uniforms were so large for us that they sagged on the ground, and most of us just ended up wearing the shirts because the pants were so baggy.

Baggy pants reminds me of when I became a boxer at age 12 or 13. When I was a kid, I never got in fights. Oh, we used to scuffle a little bit, but we didn't get mad at each other and fight. Just wrassled and played with each other for fun.

But they had a Golden Gloves boxing tournament in Greensboro that year, open class — open to anyone who could fight, and there was a novice division. So me and a Rison boy — his daddy owned a welding shop — decided we'd just enter it. Neither of us had ever been in a boxing ring.

I was so poor that I didn't even have any shorts, so I used a pair of white underwear my mother had made for me out of flour sacks and bleached white, and I bought a jockey strap for 15 cents. My mother made all my underwear out of flour sacks — they were a little rough — and she made me a shirt once in awhile, too.

Anyway, I was put in the 105-pound class and doggone if I didn't win the first fight on a decision and the next fight I won on a knockout. It was a lot of fun, really, and I didn't know until I took my gloves off that I had broke my thumb! I was supposed to fight for the championship the next night, but they wouldn't let me do it because I had that broken thumb.

All my brothers were the same way I was

then. We weren't scared to try anything. We tried whether we knew anything about it or not — we tried.

By the time I started attending Central Junior High School in the 7th grade, I had become a pretty good athlete, even if I was a little bitty skinny thing.

When I got to Greensboro High School to begin my last three years, I was 5'10" or 5'11" and weighed about 125 pounds.

By then we had moved several more times, over to Wendover again, then over to the corner of Battleground and Wharton, then over to Eugene Street, near where North State Chevrolet is now, and I had lived in six or seven places in Greensboro. We still didn't have any money, and I was often hungry.

About the only time I got a good meal was when I went to my Grandma and Grandpa's house out there at Rudd. We went maybe once or twice a month. They had fruit trees — cherry trees, pears, peaches — and they made these big cobblers and put them in a great big pan in the woodstove. They'd be two feet wide and 12 inches thick! That was the best eating I ever had. I plucked and killed many a chicken there, too.

Talk about being hungry. When I was in high school, I would wake up in the night sobbing because I was so hungry. And my stomach would be hurting and my mother would come in and rub my stomach and she'd cry. There wasn't nothing she could say but "tough times, tough times."

I didn't know it at the time, but I had a meal ticket just waiting to be punched — my athletic ability.

My mother, Blanche Welker
Dickerson, and
my brother Glenn.

My father, Raymond Dickerson (2nd from left),
with Fred (far left), me, and Herman, sometime
around 1950.

Chapter Two — Playing Ball

I had gotten pretty good playing ball over at McIver with all those kids for years, but when I first arrived at Greensboro High School, I wasn't big enough for the varsity football team, so I played on the midget team. You couldn't weigh over 125 pounds to play on it.

Frank Johnson was our coach for the midget football team. He was an ex-Marine, a short, stocky, well-built man. He had been a boxer in the Marines and I don't know that he had played much football, but they gave him that job coaching the midget team. We had a five-game schedule and that was my first organized football.

Before that I had just played sandlot football. Football was always my favorite sport and I had a knack for it, although I was pretty good at all three sports I played in high school: football, baseball, and track.

You know, back then, basketball wasn't popular like it is now and I didn't play basketball. Baseball was most popular and I usually played centerfield on the baseball team, but at times I played second base.

I was always sort of a leader on the field, and I was always a quarterback on the football team. Back then, a quarterback had to be able to run, pass, and kick, and I could do all of them.

My last two years in high school, I was big enough to play varsity football — and good enough to play three positions in the backfield — and I had Bob Jamieson as my coach. He was the same age as my brother Fred. Bob Jamieson was the man I looked up to the most in high school. He was like me and Fred — he didn't smoke, he didn't drink, and I never heard him use profanity.

My dad didn't much care about sports, other than baseball, and sports weren't as popular then as they are today. They were more or less just for the school kids, really. I don't think adults attended the high school games like they do now.

My parents never attended any of my high school games, and I don't think they ever saw any of my brothers play either — in fact, I never saw any of my brothers play. Fred and Herman were both great athletes and Herman played professional football for the Chicago Cardinals in the 1930s when I was in high school. Pro football wasn't that popular back then though and I never saw him play.

Herman started out with the Cardinals in Chicago and then the Cardinals went to St. Louis, and he played one year in each city. He was first team All-American for Sports Illustrated and was second-team All-American for UPI and AP when he was in college. He was one of the best fullbacks in the country. The other fullback that beat him out for honors was Marshall Goldburg from Pittsburgh, but they say my brother was the better all-round football player, offense and defense. He was also the best punter in the country that year. But they weren't paying him any money in the pros — I think he got a thousand dollars for signing. Today, that's just food money for a week for most pros. He told me he wasn't making anything and it was rough, so he just gave it up.

Anyway, I have good memories from my high school football days. We used what was called a double-wing, short-punt formation, with two backs on either side in the backfield, plus a tailback and a fullback. I played the tailback (quarterback) and the wingback positions and would shift from one to the other.

In those days, the rules were different. If you left the playing field for any reason — injury or substitution — you couldn't go back in until the next quarter began. So you had to go both ways, offense and defense. I played safety on defense. My job was to catch anything that went deep in the middle and to back up the halfbacks. I had a lot of territory to cover and that was one of the hardest things to do on the field.

I remember one night when we were playing Raleigh's Broughton High School at the old Riddick Stadium on the North Carolina State College campus. I was playing safety and I was getting ready to catch a punt and just as I caught it, the lights went out! They went out and I didn't know what to do, so I just stood right there, and I bet it was 30 minutes before they got them back on. They just called the ball dead right there.

Once we were playing over at High Point High School and it was real windy. I was standing on the 20-yard line and I kicked the ball and as it got up in the air a gust of wind came along and took that ball plum out of the end zone about 90 yards away. Everyone just stopped running.

Another time against Gastonia, I was running the ball from our 20-yard line and I went off between the right tackle and the end and I got in the open. I was in the clear and I wasn't looking back, of course, and I had run 70 yards when this friend of mine — his name was Pug Whitehart, he was the other halfback and he was always carrying on — he yelled, "pitch me the ball, they're gonna tackle you!" So I lateraled the ball to him on the 10-yard line and he ran it in for a touchdown. Then I looked around and there wasn't a man within 15 yards of me! He scored the touchdown and all I could say was, "What the devil!"

If I had been big enough, I would have played fullback in high school, too, but our fullback weighed about 225 and I weighed about 150. I was quick, but not fast. I was pretty good at getting off and for 10 or 15 yards, I was quick, but after that, I couldn't pump it. My specialty was quick kicks and we used a lot of quick kicks back in those days. On first, second, third down, we'd quick kick and back the other team up and use our defense. We did that many a time, kick it back on the first down. I used to practice kicking it out between the five and 10-yard lines, a coffin-corner kick. I was pretty doggone good at it.

I was pretty good at passing, too. Passing and punting. Running, I was good for 5, 10, 15 yards, but I couldn't pull it for that long distance very often.

I played football all three years at Greensboro High, and played baseball my last two years there. I ran track my last year because Coach Jamieson was wanting somebody to run high and low hurdles and he didn't have anybody on the track team who would do it. So Jabbo Johnson, our baseball coach, loaned me to Jamieson to run high and low hurdles for him! I'd never run a hurdle in my life, but I got pretty doggone good at the high hurdles. I ran them just that one year and I went to the state meet and there were two or three hundred athletes there.

They had about eight heats in the high and low hurdle runs, and I won the eighth heat. Then they had the top eight hurdlers run the finals and durn if I didn't come in third! I've never been so tickled in my life. I shocked myself. I told my brother Fred about that and he just laughed. That was in the Spring of '39 at the state meet in Chapel Hill.

Other than on the sports fields, I didn't have any goals when I was in high school. Outside school, I'd work at Hobbs Grocery for 50 cents a day — 10 hours — on the weekend. I'd gather up the groceries for people and pack'em, put stock on the shelves, get the live chickens out of their cages — we sold chickens live and whole — and tie a string around their legs and bring them in to the customers.

I had a lot of friends when I was in high school. One good friend was Aubrey Apple who I had known since I moved to Greensboro. He later became the golf pro at Green Valley Golf Course. He and I used to caddie at the Greensboro Country Club. We carried one bag at a time and got 65 cents for a whole round and if you got a dime tip or 15 cents, you were in high cotton!

Aubrey lived at the corner of Northwood and Winstead and we used to sneak over on the country club golf course — there were three holes near us. We had one wood club, one iron, and a putter, and we'd play those three holes — and get run off every time. But that's the way we learned to play golf!

One time when we were in high school,

Aubrey and I and Sted Hobbs — his brother owned the grocery store — went rabbit hunting near Sted's home on Lawndale Drive. I had my daddy's old 12-gauge shotgun and Sted had three good rabbit dogs. Sted and Aubrey and I hadn't been gone long when something started coming through the brush near us. Sted cut down on it — and killed the best dog he had! Well, I uncocked my gun and took out the shell and went home. I said, "Buddy, that's the last time I go hunting with anybody." Me and Aubrey were about 16 then and that was the only time I ever used that old 12-gauge shotgun.

Another friend was Earl Parrish who lived nearby, about 150 yards from us, and they had a big old barn and a lot of beehives back there. One day we were catching baseball in his backyard and he had a little Boston bulldog that was lying over by a tree. Earl and I were between him and the beehives. All of a sudden, every bee in all of those hives swarmed on that little dog! I could never figure out why because that dog wasn't bothering them. He wasn't within 50 feet of those hives. He was just lying by the tree, watching us catch ball.

Before we could get the hose to get the bees off of him, they'd stung him to death. He didn't die right then, but we took him up to the shed and he died there about 10 or 15 minutes later.

Sticky Burch was another good friend. He was the end on our football team. He later served with the Greensboro Police Department for many years and eventually became the county sheriff. But during our senior year in high school, Sticky and I didn't know a noun from a pronoun. A.P.

Routh, who was our principal, didn't know what to do with us, so he put us in the same special English class. Our teacher was Miss Mozell Causey. She was as sweet as could be and she told Mr. Routh, "Let me have them."

So Sticky and I were in her class. There were about 15 girls and me and Sticky. We were the only two boys in there. Every day she would send us to the board with two sentences to diagram, and neither of us knew how to diagram. But, that's what we did. We diagrammed sentences while they had class.

She loved us and we loved her, too, and those girls would get the biggest kick out of me and Sticky. Every other Monday I would bring a golden apple or a red one and put it on her desk, and the next week Sticky would do the same thing. Each day when she came to class, one of us would open the door and the other would take her by the hand and lead her into the room to her desk. Everybody loved her — she'd been there for years.

Every Friday, she'd make me and Sticky read poetry, and I'm telling you, that was a scream. Those girls would laugh! And it's a good thing they had it on Fridays because it took them a whole weekend to get over it. It was right comical and we couldn't help from laughing ourselves, because we didn't know how to read poetry. (Even to this day, 60 years later, Louise (Bateman) Sawyer — who was one of the young girls in that class— starts laughing every time she sees me.)

The week before grades would come out, Sticky and I would get a 25-cent box of candy — that was a big box then — and we'd put it on her desk. As a student, I just got by. I had mostly

C's, a very few B's, and I didn't know what an A looked like.

The best thing I remember about Miss Causey is her discipline. I remember a day that Sticky and I were at the classroom door when she started to come in and there were two boys cussing near the classroom and she lit into them. She said, "If you can't say something good, keep your mouth shut."

They started to say something back to her and Sticky and I stepped in between them and told them to get lost. They had upset her and we weren't going to stand for that. I don't use profanity and I don't like to hear anybody use it, or drinking or smoking. I'm just that way. I never heard my daddy use profanity either, although he was a heavy smoker and drank.

Another good friend I had was Jim Wolfe. Jim was a year behind me and was the fullback on the football team. He was also president of the student body and an honor student. He later played football at Duke University and served as a Marine colonel in the Pacific during World War II. He's a retired federal bankruptcy judge now. Jim had a sister named Helen and a brother named Garland. Garland later played football at Duke, too, and he now lives in Beech Mountain, N.C.

When we were in high school, I was almost like a member of his family — at least, they treated me that way. His mother, Effie, was a dietitian at a hosiery mill and his father, Boyd, worked there, too. They knew I didn't have nothing. I used to stay at their house more than I did my own. I'd go down to their house and just go in and go to

This photo, taken when I was 18 years old and a student at Greensboro High School, shows why they called me "Curly."

bed. They wouldn't even know I was upstairs asleep sometimes. I was there about every other day the last two years of high school.

At the hosiery mill, all the salesmen would give Effie hams and cakes and pies and fruits and vegetables and she'd take all that food home. I would go down in their basement and it looked like a grocery store with all those things the salesmen gave her. All the walls and ceilings had hams hanging down and she'd cook all that stuff, and I was in hog heaven!

I never did go with too many of the girls except to the school dances. We all had a few girlfriends in high school, but nothing serious. We had a real good time. I was in a sort of elite group of 25 or 30 boys and the girls had a club, too, and they would ask you to a dance. That wasn't uncommon back then. If the girls wanted an escort, they would ask a boy. They had dances every week, either at the country club or at Starmount or Sedgefield or out at Greensboro Park in a big log building there. After a ballgame and on weekends when there weren't ballgames, we'd have dances someplace.

I learned to dance from a boy named Joe Birddy. He was a good friend of mine and I knew he could dance. I asked him to teach me a few steps and he came over to the house two or three times and taught me. We used a radio to get some music. I was about 16 and I was able to jitterbug a little bit then. I even taught two or three other fellows how to dance later on.

There were about three girls I dated off and on — nothing serious — and I took one girl to the debutante ball in Raleigh. Her parents asked me to go with her. There were two chaperones for each girl. Her parents knew me. I was about as poor as they come, but I was very polite and nice to everybody and they were to me.

My brothers and I always tried to be good boys and do the right thing, and I think we were all accepted. You know, in life you have the elite — the upper class, as they say. But we always associated with everyone, from up to down. We didn't kowtow to anybody and we were well-liked and got along with everybody. That's why we got to go to debutante balls and dances, even as poor as we were.

Anyway, this girl's parents let me have their car and we drove to Raleigh for the ball. The girl had some friends there and she spent the night with them and I stayed with a fellow I knew there.

During my last year in high school, I also worked out at the swimming lake at Greensboro Country Park. Coach Jamieson got a handful of us athletes jobs out there. We'd work in the bathhouse, cleaning up, picking up towels in the dressing room, picking up trash, and doing odd jobs. I was also staying in one of the three or four log cabins up on the hill there. There was a house close by where we could go eat meals.

One Monday morning in the summer when I was staying in one of the cabins, I got up early to go do some exercising. I'd usually run around the park and then go down in front of the bathhouse to a grassy spot and exercise, squats and pushups. That was my training. We didn't have weights and didn't know what a weightroom was. We just improvised the best we knew how. We did that on our own.

Anyway, I was down on my hands and knees in that little grassy spot and I saw money all over the ground. I thought, "What in the world?" I got an old paper cup and kept picking up money — about 30-some dollars worth of change! The only thing I could figure was that a bunch of drunks must have been out there wrassling and scuffling and their money came out of their pockets.

Well, when Howard Carr, the ticket man, came in, I gave the money to him and said, "I found this out here and I have no idea who it belongs to. I thought maybe you dropped some when you left with the ticket money."

He said, "No, but I'll keep it a day or two and if nobody claims it, it's yours."

And he came and gave it to me several days later. That was in 1938.

Tying for the state co-championship in football in the fall of that year was the highlight of my senior year, but I didn't have any idea what I was going to do when I got out of school. I didn't have any goals and I wasn't intent on going to college. I wasn't really college material from the standpoint of scholastics. My grades weren't that good. I had been drug from school to school and town to town, and I didn't have a real good background. Plus, I didn't have any money.

I didn't get to go to the senior prom because I didn't have any clothes. That was probably my biggest disappointment in high school. But a lot of fellows were probably in the same boat. I didn't get a class ring or go to the prom but I did get a school sweater.

Then one day in my senior year, I got called to the office.

I thought maybe I was in trouble. I didn't know. When I got to the office, there was the coach from North Carolina State College, Doc Newton. He had been my brother Fred's football coach at Davidson College and he'd played at Davidson. He asked me if I'd be interested in going to State.

I said, "Well, I'm a little shocked. I never thought about it. I never thought about playing college football." I didn't know what to say hardly. I hadn't planned on going to college. I didn't have any clothes and I didn't have any money. I had nothing.

It turned out that a number of colleges wanted me to come play for them. Carolina contacted me and wanted me to meet a lawyer up in the Jefferson building, and I went up there two or three times and talked to him. They wanted to send me to a prep school up in Virginia, and I wouldn't go. I don't know what the story would have been there. I guess it would have been a military school where they pay for your uniforms.

Also, Presbyterian College and Virginia Tech wanted me. Four or five schools wanted me because we had a good football team — we were co-champions of the state with Durham High. We beat them during the regular season, then tied them 6-6 for the state championship. Then the next week we played the state championship team of Virginia, Roanoke, and we beat them.

It turned out that 9 of the 11 boys in our starting lineup received scholarships. The fullback — Melvin Trull — would have received one, too, but he was a junior, and one of the ends had joined the National Guard and he had to go there. Otherwise, the whole team would have gotten scholarships. We had a crackerjack ball club.

Anyway, when Doc Newton came to recruit me, he said, "How about coming down to Raleigh for a visit?" And he talked to my buddy Ray Sawyer, who was a tackle on our team. So Ray and I went down for the weekend.

Back then, all you had coaching a team were a head coach, a backfield coach, and a line coach — just three coaches. That was it. Now they have one for every position!

The line coach was Herman Hickman. He was an All-American at Tennessee and an honor student in English. He could recite poetry just like other people talk. An honor student. Of course, he didn't weigh but about 340 pounds, and he was a pro wrestler on the side.

I remember him taking us to the theater in Raleigh. We started walking down the aisle — the theater was packed — and everybody stood up and started applauding. I thought, "What in the world is going on?" I didn't know what they were applauding about. Then it dawned me that it was him they were applauding. Everybody loved him.

So, we went on upstairs to the balcony and they had a double seat up there they had made for him in the front — the very first seat.

Well, after Ray and I went to Raleigh, I figured if they wanted me, I was willing to go. They gave me a scholarship that took care of everything — meal tickets, laundry, room and board and books.

I had a fellow from Greensboro that sort of looked after me a little bit, too, while I was at State. His name was Henry Atkinson. He was an alumnus who owned a small textile mill in Greensboro down on South Elm Street.

The coaches let him know I was going there. Coach Hickman mentioned to him that I didn't have anything, no clothes or anything, and he called me up and said, "Come on over to my house." He lived off of Elm on Sunset Drive. When I got there, he gave me some money and told me to go buy myself a suit of clothes and some shoes. That was my first suit.

He'd come to State for every home game and he'd come to see me and give me $5 or so. We'd sit around and talk. I don't think he helped any of the other boys from Greensboro, though.

For the first couple of years we stayed in the field house at the end of the football field. There were bunks stacked 4-high in the rooms and I was so small that I had to sleep in a top one. But when they would get rowdy on the weekends, I would take my blanket and go to the other end of the football field and sleep down there.

Those big boys would get to drinking some and knock holes in the walls. I got away from them, never joined in.

Coach Hickman tickled me, though, when he would take two or three of those linemen over to the old Riddick Stadium and carry on with them boys, laughing and hollering, and you'd hear him all over campus. He was just jolly. He'd take the big linemen over in the gym and wrestle them — two and three at a time and nobody could beat him. That's just the way he was.

Playing football at State is where I learned my lesson about tobacco. We were practicing one day and all those big ole country boys were chewing tobacco, and I was going to be a big boy, too.

33

So, I took a chew while we were practicing off-tackle plays, cuts and blocking assignments. And I made a cut up through the middle into a bunch of them and one of those big boys hit me and I swallowed my tobacco.

I got tears in my eyes and got sick as a dog, vomited and everything else — so that cured me of tobacco. That was my sophomore year.

There were only about 2300 boys at State when I went there — and two girls. State, at that time, was an engineering, textile, and agricultural school. It wasn't a regular liberal arts or teaching college. I was in industrial arts, which included woodworking, machinery, foundry, and things like that — and, really, that didn't interest me. I just took the basic courses. I still didn't have any goals.

The two girls that were there were day students, the daughters of two of the professors. One of them was taking aeronautical engineering and the other was taking textile designing.

There were about three girls that I dated off and on while I was at State, but nothing serious. I did have one of the prettiest girl friends though. She was from Zebulon and she was the hostess at the largest restaurant in Raleigh. Her name was Ina Allen Perry and she was a black-headed beauty. She was a beauty queen in high school. I went with her a couple of years. Of course, when you go with those pretty girls, everybody is after them, and after two years, she met this fellow from Wilmington. He was at that time the assistant administrator of the hospital in Wilmington — the county hospital, the biggest in that area.

One of the nice things that happened while I was at State was that I got to see a lot of the bigtime bands. Tommy Dorsey and Frank Sinatra played for one of our dances. Woody Herman came there and Barney Rabb — we had them three nights in a row. Just about every weekend we had big bands playing in the old Thompson Gymnasium.

The fraternities had a lot of dances, too, and Doby Nelson and I were honorary members of all the fraternities. Doby was my roommate at State. He was from Maryville, Tennessee, and was a fullback on our football team. Both of us were good-natured fellows and we didn't have the money to join a fraternity, but they liked us. The fraternities gave us permission to come to any of their get-togethers, dances, or anything. We'd go to them. There were a lot of Greensboro boys at State at that time who were members of the fraternities.

Doby was a catbird. I never seen anything like him. Doby had had all of his teeth knocked out and had false teeth. We didn't have face masks for football players in those days, and just about everybody had teeth knocked out or broken noses, you name it. I never got a broken nose, but I did get kicked in the mouth one time playing in Charlotte in high school. That knocked a little piece of a middle tooth out. I spit some blood, but never got hurt. I used to take a lot of knocks. You couldn't help it with those big ole boys crushing you. You had to take it. I didn't back up from anything.

Anyway, I brought Doby to Greensboro one time in '40 to visit Jim Wolfe's sister, Helen, who worked at an insurance company in town. She was like a sister to me.

We went by and picked her up at the office and walked down Market Street to the cafe and ate lunch. We were sitting there and the waiter came and brought us a glass of water and all of a sudden that Doby took out his teeth and dropped them in the water! I like to come undone, and Helen would laugh about that everytime she would see me after that. She married and moved to Pennsylvania later and passed away just a few years ago.

Doby ate all of his food with a spoon — he was a catbird!

Except during the football season, I'd bum — thumb a ride — home and back every week or two to pick up some clothes or get them cleaned. I might have a class on Saturday morning for an hour or two, and as soon as class was over, I'd go out to Hillsboro Street and start thumbing. I'd go with whoever came by — there were quite a few boys from Greensboro, and they'd pick us up without any problem.

A couple of summers while I was at State, Ray Sawyer and I stayed on campus and worked. One summer we helped lay concrete all over the campus, working with the maintenance department. I remember laying a lot of concrete out close to the power plant near Riddick Stadium.

What I liked to do best at State, of course, was play football. Dick Watts, who was from New York, and I alternated between quarterback. We used a single-wing, the "Tennessee" system, we called it. There was a halfback, a blocking back, a fullback, and a tailback. The blocking back would call the signals and when he wasn't in there, I would call them from the tailback spot.

I played football for three years at State and had a lot of good experiences but one thing that stands out isn't a favorite memory. We were playing our big rival, the University of North Carolina, in an afternoon game and it was hot. It must have been 100 degrees or more on the field and I had played all the ballgame. They were leading us 13 to 7. Then, with less than three minutes to play, I intercepted a pass on our goal line and took it back 80 yards before a big ole lineman caught me from behind. I was so tired, but I would have crawled in a hole if there had been one to crawl in. We could have beaten them...but the game ended on the 10-yard line.

I didn't know my brother Herman was at that game — he and a friend of his had come — and I was coming off the field, so tired I could hardly walk, couldn't breathe, and my mouth was so dry I could hardly swallow — and I heard my brother say, "What's the matter? Can't you pick up your feet?"

I didn't say a word to him, I was so mad and tired. I didn't even answer him.

I had gone 80 yards before for a touchdown, but that was the second touchdown I should have scored — the other was the one I lateraled in high school — and didn't. It takes a toll having to play so long without a rest.

At the first of the season in 1941, we were playing against Mississippi State and I got all the ligaments in my knee tore up. I went off the left side and cut back between the tackle and the end, and just as soon as I did, this tackle came through

My 1940 publicity photo from North Carolina State College.

low with his shoulder pads and got me on my left knee. I was in the hospital for a month. It busted up every ligament in my knee and all they could do back then was put a screen shield-like thing over my knee with a light bulb hovering beneath it day and night, which they'd cut off sometimes.

Before the season was done, however, I was

back on the field. The last week of the football season we'd been practicing and Ray and I were walking back across the railroad tracks and through the tunnel under the fieldhouse. As we walked, I saw a bunch of fellows in white shorts with pads and sticks.

I asked Ray, "What are they doing?"

"Playing cricket," he said.

I didn't know what cricket was, but those guys were the survivors of a ship that had been torpedoed by a submarine off the coast of North Carolina near Wilmington. They were British sailors. That was when it hit me about the war.

They were letting them stay on campus for a while because they had no place to go. They had lost about half of their crew. That was the first inkling I had of the war and that was in November of 1941. Then in December the Japanese bombed Pearl Harbor.

I was 21 when the war broke out and everyone that was 18 or over had to register for the draft. I went to Greensboro as soon as I could and registered. They gave each of us a number which was put in a little capsule and then placed in a fishbowl in Washington for a lottery to see who would be drafted.

On a Saturday morning the lottery results came out in the paper and my roommate woke me up about 7 o'clock with, "Well, are you ready to go?"

"Go where?" I asked.

"They drew your number," he said.

I went on back to sleep. About an hour later I got up and looked at the paper and sure enough, Secretary Knox had drawn my number

— number 2 in the nation. I had been drafted.

This was in December and I was still in school so they deferred me until the end of the semester. In July 1942, I joined a new team.

Chapter Three — Joining a new team

After I was drafted, I had the choice of picking a branch of the service or just going to whatever branch they sent me. About that time, in May and June of '42, the Army was forming an ordinance company in Greensboro. Joe Carruthers, a lawyer, and George Roach, who used to be mayor, and an insurance man named George Underwood were in charge of forming the company in Guilford, Randolph, and Rockingham counties.

I knew a lot of those fellows so I joined the 302nd Army ordinance company in July. We were sent to Ft. Jackson, South Carolina, for about a week to get our uniforms and shots. Then they shipped us all the way to Ft. Lewis, Washington, to study ammunition, demolition, booby traps, and all kinds of weapons. Joe Carruthers was our commander and he was a captain or major at that time.

I guess the hardest thing for me to adapt to about the military was getting up so early — 5 o'clock in the morning. We had KP (kitchen patrol) and other duties, too, cleaning up the latrine and floors and things like that. Of course, except for getting up early, none of that was too unusual for me because I'd been cleaning house all my life since I was 6 or 7. I'd chopped kindling, brought in the coal, taken out the ashes, and helped with other chores. When mother and daddy were working, I was taking care of the house mostly because I was the youngest one and the other boys were away. I had washed dishes after every meal, made the bed, swept the floor — and I still do today!

I wasn't crazy about the military, though, and at first it was kind of a shock because I didn't know what to expect. Of course, living in the South all my life and then going to other places, it was sort of a funny feeling. Away from home all of a sudden and getting used to the military, not knowing from one day to the next where you were going to be, that was the hard part about it.

Ft. Lewis was a big place with over 100,000 troops, not too far from Seattle. That meant plenty of men for football games, however, and there were 7 teams at that fort. I became captain of one of them and played quarterback. Our team became the champions of Ft. Lewis.

Of course, we weren't there to play football but to learn about ordinance. We would train during the day and then practice football in the afternoons. The ordinance companies supplied weapons and equipment for all branches of the Army. Before I joined the Army, however, I had no experience with weapons. I went hunting one time with my daddy's 12-gauge shotgun and I didn't even fire it. That was when Sted Hobbs killed his own dog. I knew nothing at all about weapons.

At Ft. Lewis we went to the rifle range and learned how to throw a grenade, too. As far as learning about weapons, we started off with the Springfield '03, which we didn't use very long. Then we went to the carbine, a slow .30-caliber rifle with a short barrel and a little magazine. Then we went to the M-1, a larger rifle. Then we learned the BAR (Browning Automatic Rifle) and the .30-caliber machine gun. I didn't actually operate all of those, just learned about them. Also the 81 mm mortar and the anti-tank guns, and the shells.

I had been at Ft. Lewis for about two months when I was told to report to the office. A Colonel Gavin wanted to speak to me on the phone.

Colonel James M. Gavin was a friend of my brother, Herman, who was now a major in the paratroopers. I believe Herman was in the 501 Regiment but I don't know if it was part of the 101st Airborne or what. He had been in the ROTC at Virginia Tech before the war and had been in the reserves as an officer, and they called him to active duty when the war broke out. He was working at a bank at the time. Anyway, Gavin knew him from the summer reserve camps and he asked the reserve officers to recommend athletes for a special unit and Herman recommended me.

When I got on the phone with Colonel Gavin he told me who he was and that he had talked to my brother, and that he wanted 50 good athletes to volunteer for a special group in a paratrooper outfit — but he didn't say what they would be doing.

I told him, "Well, Colonel, I ain't never been in an airplane, much less jumped out of one!"

We talked awhile and then he said, "Let me know in a couple of days."

Well, what I was doing at Ft. Lewis was a little dull and I wanted to get into something a little more exciting than ordinance. I'm not rubbing that job or any job in the service, but I thought, "What have I got to lose?" So, I called him back in a couple of days.

I was the only person out of the ordinance unit to go. Colonel Gavin had also picked people from anti-aircraft and tank units, from communications and artillery, from the motor pool, and so forth. He had picked a group of men that could do anything and among them could speak 14 languages. Most of the guys were from the North and West — all the way from California, Oklahoma. We had Italian boys, Polish boys, Czechs — we were made up of immigrants, just like the United States is. There was only one Rebel in the group and that was me.

It wasn't long before they were teasing me because I couldn't speak another language. "Come on, speak a different language for us," they'd say.

And I'd say, "Well, I can speak one — the Southern USA type — 'y'all.'"

One of Colonel Gavin's requirements had been that the men couldn't be over 6 feet tall and 170 pounds — he wanted small, lean, rugged, and not-so-heavy men. If they were too heavy, their weight would blow panels out of the silk parachutes they were using then. Later on, of course, we used nylon chutes.

I was about 165 pounds by then and 5'11" tall — one of the largest men in the group. Most weighed between 140 and 165 pounds.

All the men selected were sent to Ft. Benning, Georgia. Colonel Gavin was the regimental commander of the 505th PIR (Parachute Infantry Regiment) of the 82nd Airborne. General Matthew Ridgway was the commanding general of the 82nd, and a Colonel Tucker was the head of the 504th PIR with the 82nd.

The Airborne had been started on March 25 of that year with generals Bradley and Ridgway and they had broken it into two divisions, the 101st Airborne and the 82nd Airborne. The 101st was sent to Kentucky.

When we first met with Colonel Gavin at Ft. Benning, we were all sort of in awe. Most of us still didn't know much about the military and we were meeting with a colonel, and we didn't have any idea what he had in mind. He talked to the 50 of us and just one other officer.

At that first meeting, he said that he was forming a new squad, but he didn't tell us what kind of squad or what name we would have. He said, "You will not tell anybody about your training, what you are doing, or where you are going, or anything." Nobody was supposed to know anything about us — except the officers and sergeants training us — we were just a regular class as far as anyone knew.

The first week there our training was just like everybody else's. Marching, all kinds of exercise, beginning with a 5-mile jog every morning, no equipment. After breakfast, we would have an hour briefing about paratrooping. Then there would be classes during the day — learning to tumble, wrestle, climb ropes.

Climbing ropes in the hangar was the hardest thing for me. I could do anything else, but I could hardly do that, climb those ropes straight up to the top of the hangar. Some of those guys would go up like monkeys. I would finally make it up and down, but I just didn't have the knack of holding that rope and using my arms and legs at the same time to get up it. The rope was several inches thick without any knots to hold and was probably 30 feet high.

We also did a lot of tumbling from various towers, beginning with a 35-foot high tower and going up to a 250-foot tower. On the short tower, you would come down a rope on a little pulley and release yourself, hit the ground, and tumble forward and roll. If you did that right, it didn't make any difference what you landed on, it wouldn't hurt.

We'd climb up the back of the 35-foot towers, but on the big one, they'd draw us up on a platform. On the big tower, we used a regular parachute that was already open, and they would drop us harnessed into it. You'd hit and tumble. Usually into sawdust pits.

They also had a mock airplane that was two or three feet off the ground. We began our practice jumping out of it and tumbling into a sawdust pit. They took us up in steps.

I was a bit leery of all this, never having been through it before. I was always a little tense, but there was lots of repetition and we got stronger and stronger. We also had to learn how to pack our own parachutes before we did our five qualifying jumps. We had to pack our own chutes for all five of those jumps.

They had large tables about three to four feet wide and about 30 feet long where we learned how to fold the chutes and put them in the pack. We all had to do that but it wasn't hard to do. If you get them in there correctly, folded and rolled up, there is a piece on the back of the pack that you tie a string from to the apex of the parachute. When those are tied together and you go out of the plane, you're connected to a cable which pulls the chute out. It breaks the string. You just had to be sure that you tied those strings right to the pack and the chute.

After our first five jumps, there were riggers who packed our chutes. That was their only job in the service: pack chutes. And they were good at it. They didn't mess around.

We made our five qualifying jumps in our fourth week of training. We were supposed to make one on each day that week. We jumped on Monday, Tuesday, and Wednesday, but there was bad weather for the next two days, and we had to make two jumps on Saturday.

Strangely enough, my first jump wasn't bad at all. I didn't hesitate. They took us up about five or six men at a time with instructors with us. We stood in the plane door over the drop zone and they would slap us on the back of the leg, telling us, "Go!"

That first day we were jumping, there was a boy in front of me and he froze in the door. I'd never seen that happen before, of course, and it took four of us to get him away from the door, one on each arm and one on both legs, and we had a time pulling him back. They would give you a chance to do it again, but if you didn't want to jump, you didn't have to jump. But, after you'd made your five jumps and qualified for the paratroopers, they could court martial you if you didn't jump after that.

Anyway, we got him away from the door and I was next and I didn't hesitate at all. It didn't bother me in the least. Of course, I was always tense when I jumped, I guess everybody was. The worst thing for me about jumping was taking off in the durn airplane, getting off the ground. Those planes would shake and rattle and roll, and purr and moan and groan, and I'd be thinking, "I hope it gets off the ground!" But once we were in the air, no problem.

When we made our first jumps, we just had a helmet and two chutes, but no weapons. I thought it was great on that first jump, floating down and looking around. I'd never been in an airplane in my life until the day I jumped out of that one. It was real pretty weather that day.

On other jumps, sometimes fellows would end up walking around on top of your parachute. I did it and other fellows did the same thing, but you had to be careful. You have to get off from up there because you're taking up all the draft coming up and his chute will collapse if you don't get off. So, fellows would yak and talk a lot and then get off.

We jumped from about 1200 feet for our first five jumps, and after a month at Ft. Benning, I was officially a paratrooper at the end of September 1942. But it was October before Colonel Gavin met with us again, after we had finished jump school.

He still didn't tell us what were going to do or be, but he sent 40 of us to Camp Claiborne, Louisiana. He didn't give us any information about why we were training but he told us again not to tell anyone.

We started every morning with a 5-mile run. Then we'd have our breakfast and clean our weapons. We all carried a .38 pistol with a silencer and we had a knife. We also had something nobody else knew about — we called it a pick. It was like an ice pick but the blade was about 12 inches long with a little handle. The blade was about as big around as the end of a little finger with three edges sharp enough to shave with. We carried the knives and picks in sheathes, one outside each boot.

We also had .45-caliber Thompson machine guns — Tommy guns. Each magazine held 30 bullets and we carried three magazines on one side of our body and three on the other, and three in our backpacks. We carried plenty of ammunition.

We also carried our rations, but most of the time we didn't carry a blanket. We were taught that in combat you could rip open your chute after you jumped and landed, cut the shrouds off and put it in your pack for a blanket. It was warmer than a blanket and you could sleep in 10-degree weather with it.

Everyone wore compasses and four men had binoculars. Everyone carried maps, too, and we all learned how to read them. Plus, we had our regular equipment, like canteens, knives, watches, backpacks, pencil and paper, first aid kits, and field phones.

We had all this equipment, but we didn't know what we were training to do yet. We'd go out to the rifle range and use our Tommy guns, getting into different positions, lying flat sometimes, on knees sometimes, standing up sometimes.

We would have "problem" training in the daytime and at night, learning how to find our way to a spot and find our way back. We learned to read terrain. And we learned about the moon and stars, using them for general directions at night so we could find our way, moving silently.

When we practiced combat, we were taught to stay about five yards apart, staggered, and to fire low. I don't know what the range was on our Tommy guns, because they were training us for close-encounter fighting, waiting until the target was within 10 or 15 yards of us.

We made about a half-dozen jumps while we were at Camp Claiborne, half at daytime, half at nighttime.

The night jumps were just like the others, just another jump. The pilots were so good. They were about the top pilots in C-46s and C-47s. They could read our drop zones pretty well. Whereas, you take the other division jumps with so many airplanes and pilots, so many times they missed the drop zones. But those pilots at Camp Claiborne, they hit those drop zones just about on the dot every time. We used red and green lights on the plane to tell us when to jump. The red light stayed on until the pilot turned on the green jump light. When the green went on, we jumped.

We made those jumps from a very low altitude, so no one carried a backup parachute because there wouldn't be time to use it anyway. Our squad used two planes flying at different levels — one at maybe 600 feet and the other behind at 700 feet so he could see what was going on, so we would all hit pretty close together. And we hit those drop zones pretty doggone good, those pilots were so good.

We were all still privates as we were going

through the training, but Gavin had kind of put me in charge of the group. I had been one of the tops in almost everything we did — shooting, calisthenics, and so forth. So he just put me in charge.

We were coming back at the end of one training day and one of the fellows — Jake, an American Indian from Oklahoma — had been agitating and carrying-on. He was one of those kind who are smart-talking, a "you don't know what you're doing and I can do it better" type. An agitator. Since early on in training he had been making sarcastic remarks about me, for a couple of weeks, and I had sort of been ignoring it, but that day before we got back to the camp area, I just stopped the group. I told all the fellows, "Make a circle and take off all of your equipment, and sit down on the ground."

Then I called Jake out there and said, "Jake, let's you and me settle something here and now. You've been agitating and carrying-on and" — and about that time, he took a swing at me.

Well, it's the only real fight I ever got into in my life. We went at it for a pretty good while there, bar nothing. Wrassling, hitting, boxing, whatever you want to call it. I knew that he wasn't in too good a shape because he was a right heavy smoker and he liked to drink, too, and I didn't do either. He came at me real low finally and I hit him with an uppercut in his right eye and he went down like a shot!

So, I told the fellows to drag him over to a tree and take their canteens and pour their water on him. He was plum out. After we revived him, we went on back to the camp. The next morning we got up and fell out for roll call, and I had never seen such an eye as his in my life. It looked like it was going to fall out on the ground. It was so closed and bruised and black and blue, that he couldn't even see out of it.

The officer that was in charge of us looked at him and kind of laughed to himself and then said, "Go on up to the messhall and get a beefsteak to put on that eye."

After that, Jake was my best buddy. He stuck with me like glue and stopped agitating, and was sort of my body guard after that.

We were at Camp Claiborne for two months before Colonel Gavin called us together at the end of that training and told us what we were going to be. There were 30 of us that he talked to and he told us, "You're a special unit and you'll operate behind enemy lines." Well, of course, we all kind of looked at each other...and it still didn't sink in. You know, we had all been civilians just a few months earlier. But what he told us pretty much explained one thing they had been teaching us at Camp Claiborne. They had taught us how to silence guards.

They taught us to do that in teams of three. rather than just one man doing it, because you didn't know if just one man could handle a guard. Each of the three men had an assignment and was called the Number 1, Number 2, or Number 3 man. Number 1 would grab the guard's weapon and pull it real quick out away from him, Number 2 would grab him around the mouth and pull his head back, and Number 3 was the stabber — he would take that pick and stick the guard right through the rib cage. It would glance off the ribs and go into the heart from the side, and it beat slitting somebody's throat where you'd get blood all over you. I was usually the Number 3 man. All three men would lay the guard down quietly after we had killed him.

We called our special 30-man unit the "hit squad."

When we got ready to leave Camp Claiborne, I was made an acting staff sergeant and three other guys — Arnie, Bob, and Gary — were made acting sergeants.

Arnie was a Polish boy from New York. He could speak Polish, German, Italian. He was a typical Yankee — ran his mouth all the time — but a good communications man, good on the field telephone. We had one field phone and we had two runners we could use if we lost communications. Jake, the Indian boy, was one of them. The other was a little Italian boy from New Jersey. We called him "Slick" because he had slick black hair. He was a dark-skinned little thing who was good at gambling, so everybody called him Slick.

Bob was a Polish boy, too, a pretty quiet boy from West Virginia. He was an 81 mm mortar man. He was real quiet, not obnoxious, real likable. He could speak German, Polish, and I think some Czech.

Gary, now, he was one of those kinds that was always into something. If there were any civilians around — any women — well, he was going to go after them women. That's the kind he was, a womanizer. He was the lover-boy of our group, but he didn't get to do too much about that. He was an orphan from Michigan, and he had played a lot of football in high school.

So, I became an acting staff sergeant in charge of the others and the other three men were made acting sergeants under me. I didn't have to handle 30 men by myself with the other three sergeants to handle small groups of them.

Gavin told us, "When you leave here, we're going to separate you. You'll be put two or three together in various companies in the 505th regiment, and I'll call you together when we get overseas. In the meantime, you tell no one what you've been trained to do."

That was around the last of November when we finished up at Camp Claiborne. We then went to Ft. Bragg, North Carolina, where the 82nd Airborne had gone, and that was when I got my first leave, a three-day pass. I got my pass and I hurried to the bus station.

The bus was pulling out into the street when I got there and the driver saw me. He asked me if I was going to Greensboro and I said yes, and he said, "Go get your ticket."

Back then gas and automobile tires and so forth were rationed, so lots of people traveled by bus. When I got on the bus, it was plum full and I had to stand back towards the back. I was standing beside these two young girls who were sitting in a seat and I started talking to the one who was next to me. The girl on the other side was looking out the window and I could tell that she was mad at something, but I didn't know what. She didn't even look at me, but I kept talking to the other girl until we got to Greensboro.

I found out that she had come down to visit her boyfriend at Ft. Bragg and had brought her friend, the girl who was looking out the window. They were from Huntington, West Virginia, and as soon as they'd gotten to Ft. Bragg, they'd had to turn around and leave because she got word that her grandfather had died. That's the reason the other one was mad, because she had to turn around and go back. She was wanting to visit down there, too, even though she didn't have a boyfriend there.

Well, when we got to Greensboro, they couldn't make a connection on to Huntington. My mom and dad lived on Eugene Street, about four blocks from the bus station which was on Gaston Street, so I said, "Why don't y'all just come on down to my house and spend the night and catch the bus tomorrow morning?" So they did. My mother didn't mind and she welcomed them.

Joanne Altizer was the girl I had been talking to. The other was named Edna Lee Kearns, and when she got off the bus, that was the first time I ever really saw her face. She was a nice-looking girl and well-built.

They spent the night at my home and left the next day. We had gotten there in the late afternoon and we all went to bed about 10 o'clock, and I didn't really have much time to talk to Edna Lee. So I started corresponding with her.

When I got back to Ft. Bragg, I was still in training — going to the rifle ranges, learning the weapons. We had a few more jumps — I had 19 jumps altogether in training. Not a lot, but nobody else had a lot at that time either.

In my company in the 505th regiment, there were only three of us from the special unit that had trained at Camp Claiborne — me and the two runners, Jake and Slick. The rest of the men were in other companies, two or three to a company.

When I wasn't working with the hit squad, I was part of a machine gun platoon. We used a .30-caliber belt-fed machine gun on a tripod and I could do any of the jobs associated with it — gunner, ammunition carrier, anything.

In the hit squad we didn't carry a rifle, just the Tommy guns, which would be issued secretly when we got called together. Gavin had it all set up to not let too many people know what we would be doing. When we would get back from a mission, they would take away our Tommy guns, our picks, and other special equipment. In my regular unit, I used a carbine. It was the easiest thing to carry around.

We did a heckuva lot of walking and running and exercises while we were at Ft. Bragg. It was nothing unusual for us to go on a 25 or 30-mile hike. Then, near the end of March and beginning of April 1943, every day for two solid weeks, we'd put full gear on and we'd go out 12 miles, eat, and turn around and come back — 24 miles.

They kept us a little harassed doing those things, and men would be griping about having to do all that walking, but that wasn't nothing unusual. I guess I never found the training to be all that hard. I think one of the biggest things was going from civilian life into the military and learning to take orders. When you get all those people together, different personalities, it's a little hard. That was one of the hardest things — discipline. But I had been learning that since I was

Life was sweet and I was sweet on Lee. This photo was taken on April 12, 1943, the day after we were married.

a kid.

    Sometime around the first week of April, after they'd stepped up the training, I had an inkling that we were getting ready to go overseas and I called Edna Lee and asked her if she wanted to marry me. I hadn't seen her but that one time when she was on her way back to Huntington, but I had written her every week since then and had called her about once a week. She said "Yes" when I asked.

I got a three-day pass and went to Huntington. That was the first time I had met her parents. I'm sure they were surprised and didn't know what to think or say. But Lee — that's what I called her — was never bashful about saying what she wanted to do, and they didn't question her when she said she was going to get married.

It was the second time I'd seen her, but I wasn't nervous. I'm one of these guys that's never been too nervous or excited about too much.

I wore my uniform and we went to Catlettsburg, Kentucky, which is just a little ways from Huntington. We were married April 11, 1943.

We stayed at her parents home for two days and then I returned to Ft. Bragg.

Before the month was over, I was headed overseas to war.

Chapter Four — Fighting in Sicily

Exactly one month after I married Edna Lee Kearns, I found myself in Casablanca. I hadn't seen her since our marriage. Around the first week in May, the 82nd Airborne had boarded ship in New York harbor and sailed for North Africa. We were going to be part of the invasion of Sicily, although we didn't know it yet.

From Casablanca we went to Oujda in French Morocco, near the border of Algeria. For the next two months we acclimated ourselves to the desert weather there and its 100-degree temperatures. When we tried to eat, we had to cover our food because the sand would blow in it. Mostly we just stayed in tents out in the desert. It was boring. We did some exercises but not much else, although we did make one practice jump which never should have been made.

A bunch of dignitaries — including General Eisenhower and the Sultan of Morroco and maybe a dozen more — were there and wanted to see a jump. The day we jumped there wasn't any breeze stirring when we left the airfield, but by the time we got up there to make the jump, about a 35 mph wind came up and they didn't call us back. Normally you don't jump if the wind is more than 8 miles an hour, but we jumped. When I hit, my parachute dragged me along the ground for a hundred yards before I could collapse it, and I had scratches all over my hands and face from the sand. But I was lucky. We had men with broken necks, arms, and legs. We had a lot get hurt that day, and that was the only jump we made before

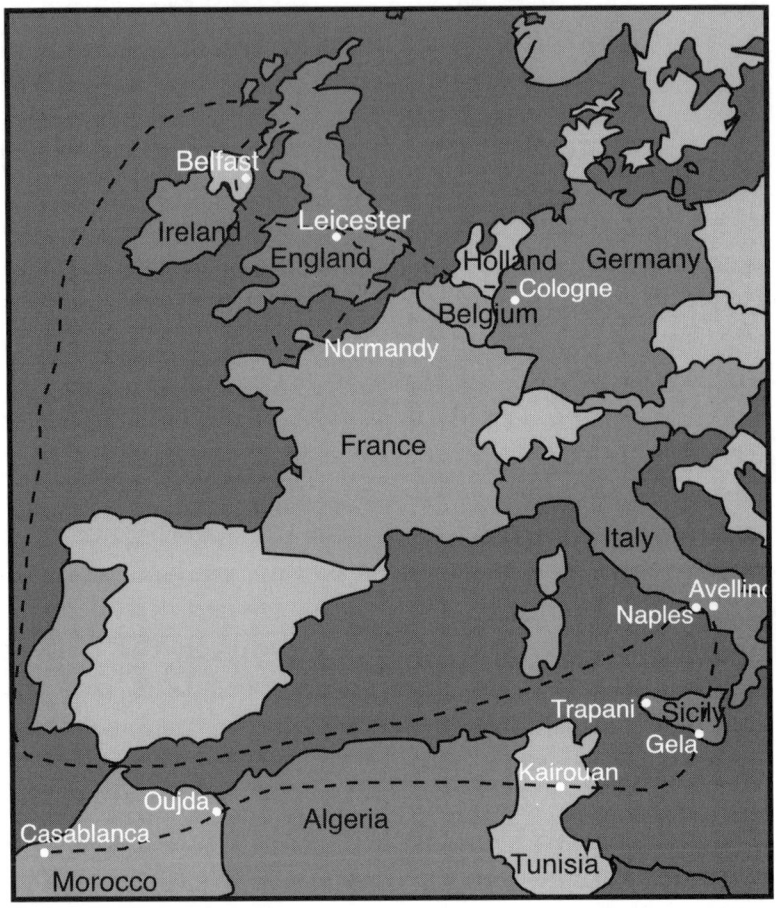

This map shows the wide-ranging area that the 82nd Army Airborne (including me and my hit squad) covered during World War II.

---

we made our first combat jump in Sicily, just on the other side of the Mediterranean.

Our base for our jump into Sicily was at Kairouan, Tunisia, where we went the first week of July. At Kairouan, we stayed at an oasis where camels and horses came to drink in the desert. They had fruit trees there but there was no camp there. We just set up among all those trees, pitched little mosquito nets under the trees, and we wore shorts the whole time. It was about 110 degrees during the day, too hot to do anything. After about 9 o'clock in the morning, you didn't go anywhere until it started to get dark again, except to get something to eat at mealtime.

I remember going up to the medical unit one day and I looked up under the trees there and I bet there were 50 guys laid out with heat prostration, and they had messed all over themselves. That weather would kill you.

During the two months we'd been in North Africa, our hit squad had not been called together. Our regimental headquarters kept a list of our group and a Major Martin and a Captain Swain were in charge and oversaw the 30 of us. When we got to Kairouan, our 30-man team was called together for a briefing and we learned that we were going to be leading the way, jumping into Sicily. We soon received a second briefing, and then Colonel Gavin and I were part of a briefing with generals Bradley, Patton, Clark, Montgomery, and Ridgway, along with Colonel R. H. Tucker.

Reconnaissance planes had flown over the island and taken pictures. Then nine Intelligence teams had worked over those photographs every day for a week, and had everything diagrammed on a large sand table — streams, rivers, high ground, airfields, munitions, factories. Anything they had pictures of, they put on that table.

There were two airfields close to Gela, northeast of it. Our hit squad was given the objective of taking one of those airfields so that it could be used by our air force to bring in supplies. Our mission was to capture the airfield and destroy the Messerschmidt fighter airplanes that were on the runways there.

Meeting with all of those generals and colonels didn't bother me in the least. Gavin had briefed me real well about what we were going to do and it was all on that table. I told them what we would be doing and they followed it. After all those dignitaries had left, we brought the rest of our 30 men in for their third briefing, this time with the pictures taken by the reconnaisance planes.

After Major Martin and Captain Swain had our parachutes and other equipment sent to us by two trucks and we'd had our briefings, we were ready to go. You know, we really hadn't been together that long, just training together for several months the latter part of '42. We hadn't been together since then and we hadn't had much time to learn much about each other and the next thing we knew, we were going into combat.

We went out to the airstrip about six hours before takeoff time and had our final briefing right on the airstrip. We were briefed on our drop zone again and what we were supposed to do. We checked over all our equipment two or three times. After everything was squared away, we played cards for a little while to relax and talked a little bit, and then there was silence before we boarded the plane. Nobody said a word, but everybody knew what they were supposed to do.

The rest of the 505th regiment was at another airstrip not far from us and would be following behind us several hours later. We took off at 8 o'clock on the night of July 9, 1943, headed for Gela, Sicily.

My first concern was getting off the ground. I always gritted my teeth on a takeoff. We were in C-46s or C-47s — cargo planes — good airplanes, tough, but they shook, rattled, and rolled. They were the workhorses of the services and we had the best pilots you could get. They were part of the 52nd Troop Carrier Wing of the Army Air Corps. We were in two planes, 15 men in each.

Other than the noise of the planes, there was silence. We were all a little nervous and tense. Everyone was a little edgy and didn't want to talk. A few may have said something, but I didn't pay much attention. Several sort of dozed or closed their eyes, trying to relax. Each of us handled it our own way.

By 10:00 p.m., we were over our drop zone about three miles from the Gela airfield. Meanwhile, Colonel Gavin and the rest of the troops of the 505th were taking off back in Kairouan and all of them would be off the ground by 11 p.m. They were to fly east and swing back over Malta and come in on the south coast of Sicily. We were to find our way to them after we completed our mission.

Coming in over the island, our Navy was bombarding the coast and it looked like fireworks going on there. Gela was inland from the coast, and as we came in on our drop zone, one plane was flying at 600 feet and the other was right behind it at 700 feet.

I was the lead jumper, the jump master, and we would be the first American airborne to touch foreign soil in combat. I guess you could call that an honor, I don't know.

We jumped and landed right where we expected to, about three miles from the airfield. It had only taken us about 20 seconds to hit the ground from 600 or 700 feet, and it only took about three minutes for the 30 of us to assemble. Even though it was dark, it wasn't that hard to see, and I had an infrared light we used to help us assemble.

We started working our way towards the airfield, stopping along the way at a couple of farm houses. At each house, we surrounded it, and then I took Slick, who could speak Italian, and Arnie who spoke German, and knocked on the door to rouse whoever was in the house. At each house, a man answered the door, and we told each of them not to be afraid, that we were Americans and we wanted information. We wanted to know what was covering the airfield and barracks — how many sentries were at the airfield and how many soldiers — and they told us, no problems. They were willing to help and we learned where the guards would be.

We also told these farmers that 30,000 American paratroopers had landed, which wasn't true — only about 3,000 had landed — but we wanted the Italians and Germans to think there were a lot of us there, and we wanted the civilians to get that information out. They did, too, and within a few hours, Italian radio was reporting that 100,000 Americans had landed! Most of the Italians, it seemed, had relatives in the United States and they didn't really want to fight us.

As we worked our way to the airfield, we stayed at the edge of the woods along the road, which was a secondary type of road. We had one man watching our rear and two out on each side, and several times we stopped and put our ear to the road to see if we could hear any vehicles or troops on the road ahead. But we didn't have any problems. It took us about two hours to make the three miles to the airfield, but by midnight, we were there.

There were eight guards around the airstrip and we divided up into eight threesomes to take care of them. I sent the six remaining men in our squad over to the one barracks that was there, just in case anything went wrong with the guards. Those six had the barracks covered with one man on each side and two men at both the front and back in case anyone started out or heard anything.

We gave ourselves 30 minutes to take care of the guards and then to meet outside the barracks. Arnie and Bob and I went together to take care of one of the guards. I was the Number 3 man, the stabber, and I did it. That was the first time, and I had sort of a numb-like feeling, but I shrugged it off. I didn't look at his face. He was just a blank to me. Later I thought about it. You know, stabbing somebody like that — I had never dreamed I'd have to do something like that, but in war you do things you don't think you're ever going to have to do.

After the first time or two, and after seeing atrocities and all — what's been done to soldiers and civilians and livestock and property — you don't think too much about it.

Anyway, everything went smoothly with all of the guards, and when all 30 of us were back together, we surrounded that barracks. I had a small flare gun and when I fired it over the barracks, one man on each side of the barracks threw a stick of dynamite with a short fuse into the windows, or under the barracks if they couldn't get it in a window — and that thing blew to pieces. There must have been 100 pilots and mechanics in there and nobody came out. Nobody.

After we had taken care of the men in the barracks, we ran along the runway where there were about a dozen Messerschmidts, pitching grenades in the cockpits and blowing up the instrument panels. We didn't have to blow the whole plane up. It hadn't taken us long to do what we had to do at Gela, destroy the planes and the barracks. Less than an hour, and we hadn't lost a man.

When we finished up at Gela, we started working our way back to where Colonel Gavin and the rest of our troops were supposed to be coming in along the south coast. It turned out that Colonel Gavin and the small group who had jumped from his plane had landed about 30 miles off the drop zone. We didn't run into much opposition and before mid-morning, July 10, we ran across Gavin. He had picked up a few other men along the way and all of us started up one of the few main highways that led north from the coast, headed to a nearby place called Biazzo Ridge, where we would meet up with our men in the 505th Regiment.

We got there about 10 o'clock. Although we knew that Hermann Goerring's armored division was in that area, we didn't know where they were, and so we started out across the big olive orchard on Biazzo Ridge. We were about halfway across the orchard when three tanks ran in on us. We were scattered out across that field, about five or six yards apart and didn't have a thing to knock those tanks out. We had some bazookas, but when they were tried, the shells just bounced off the tanks. Didn't do any good, did nothing. We were pinned down and those tanks were ripping us apart.

I was part of a group of nine men who laid down along the ditch beside a fence along the little road that ran through the orchard. The fence was just a few wires strung across, and there was just a little brush along it, but not enough to hide. The tanks came through the orchard with their machine guns blazing and shooting their 88 cannons point blank, and with soldiers following them. There was nothing we could do but scurry — we couldn't get up and run.

I was lying there as one of the tanks came up on us and killed the eight men in front of me with its machine guns. I heard them groan when they were hit and I was lying there with my head sideways watching the tank come right at me. I was plum petrified. I couldn't move. The tank came within three feet of me, mashing men in front of me, after ripping them apart with machine gun fire.

I tell you that was a monstrous thing. He could have run over me if he'd wanted to, but I guess he thought he'd gotten me. That was the first time I've ever been truly scared. That was it.

The tank turned and went out over the field and there were other fellows lying out there and the tank ran right over some of them before the three tanks pulled back. Then three

67

Messerschmidts came in and strafed all of us who were pinned down in that no-man's land. They made three runs at us before they moved out, only to be followed by three bombers that came in and laid bombs on us. I was bouncing on the ground, and they just tore us up. We couldn't move.

That lasted until about 4:30 that afternoon when the 45th Infantry Division arrived with three howitzers and two anti-tank guns and knocked all three tanks out. About that time, I crawled out across the field and checked some of the fellows and so many of them were just body parts laid out all over the place. One of my friends was over a machine gun and I picked his head up and they had got him right between the eyes.

Of the 180 men there, about 120 were wounded. We had 45 killed, eight of them my men. It didn't upset me too much at that time seeing all of that. There's nothing much you can do about it — just try to protect yourself and your men. Later on, it caught up with a lot of the men, but I lasted pretty good until after I got out of the service. I still think about it now and have flashbacks. Always have, always will. Can't help it.

So, all of that happened the first 24 hours I was in Sicily. We got back with our regular company — Headquarters Company, 3rd Battalion, 505th Regiment — that day and after the next seven or eight days, there wasn't much more combat, just cleaning up actions. It took 16 days to complete the mission in Sicily, but all of it wasn't combat. The Germans were retreating, leaving about 25,000 Italian troops who surrendered — the Italians didn't want to fight to begin with.

The Germans moved over to the boot of Italy

and left the Italians in Sicily holding the bag, and they surrendered in droves, along with some of the Germans in charge of them. They fought a delaying action most of the time with their snipers pinging at us. You couldn't see them in the trees or bushes or houses. That's how I got it on the 14th day in Sicily.

When I got hit, we were spread out, moving towards Trapani. I was stepping over a log when a sniper shot at me and hit a grenade I had in my right pants pocket. The grenade exploded and blew the pants off my leg. It blew holes in my calf and thigh. I wasn't bleeding a lot though, and I picked a great big hunk of the grenade — the top part where the pin is — out of my leg. (Twenty years later, I would still be picking little pieces out of my leg as they worked themselves to the surface. I'd be sitting and feel an itching, find a little pimple, prick it, and a piece of metal the size of a pinhead or so would come out.)

I could hardly walk after the grenade exploded, but I could hobble. Finally, two days later, they sent me back to a hospital in North Africa.

Chapter Five — Fighting in Italy

I don't even know where that hospital was, but it must have been in Morocco. I didn't do anything there for about three weeks. Finally, those of us that could maneuver — and I could get around fairly well — were put out in a tent city, even though we were still all bandaged up.

When you get hurt like that and they send you to a hospital, 99% of the time you don't go back to your outfit. They put you somewhere else. I didn't know that until we got out to the tent city and some fellow told me. I don't know who he was because I wasn't that close to anybody there, but when he told me that, I thought: they ain't gonna do that to me. I'm not going to let them send me to no hole in the wall or some place like that.

So I went AWOL (absent without leave) from the hospital. I just walked away. I had some clothes and there was an airstrip not too far away, so I bummed me a ride there. I talked to a couple of pilots and asked them if they were going to Sicily, and they said, "Yeah." I said, "How about a ride?"

I rode in the nose of a B-25 bomber for a thousand miles at about 13,000 feet, and there was a hole in the nose part where I was sitting, where the machine gun was. I didn't have a leather jacket, just my khakis, and I liked to have froze to death! It was so cold and that airplane made more durn racket than you ever heard in your life. I couldn't hear for two days after that.

But I got back to Sicily, and I asked around

as to where the 82nd Airborne was and durned if they weren't close to where I had landed. So I bummed a ride and went back to my unit. I got back with all the bandages still on my leg, and still hobbling. That was about September 10, and two or three days later, we were jumping into Italy.

Mark Clark's 5th Army had invaded Italy a day or two before we jumped and they were about to get pushed into the sea. Our hit squad only had 22 men now and they gave us another night mission, jumping behind the lines at Salerno. Our objective was to destroy some trucks full of weapons and ammunition at Avellino.

That was one of the prettiest nights we ever had for a jump. It was a full moon, a beautiful night. We jumped not too far from the little town of Avellino. When you're coming down, of course, most of the time you can guide your chute if you can see, but I wasn't paying much attention to it. I was looking down and I saw a lot of objects below in the field. They were cows, but before I realized it, I had landed on one just as pretty as you've ever seen. There must have been a hundred cows in that field and the one I landed on started mooing, and so did the rest. I guess that was the funniest jump I ever had, if you want to call it funny. All the guys landed in that big pasture, but I was the only one that landed on a cow. I sat there for a second or two and slid off. I could try that another hundred times and never do it again.

We weren't far from our objective, maybe two or three miles. We had tried to get as close as we could because there was already fighting going on around there. We started working our way in and, just like in Sicily, we stopped at a few houses. The people were so scared they didn't know what to do, but we told them we weren't going to hurt them, they just needed to give us information. They knew exactly how many guards and trucks there were.

The guards at Avellino were walking their posts when we got there, and they were the only soldiers there. The other troops must have been fighting on the coast. We were in our three-man teams and we just waited until the guards stopped and made their pivots and had their backs to us. There were four of them and we took care of them as quickly as we could — went right at it as soon as we got there, and it didn't take us more than two or three minutes. We got rid of them the same way we'd done the ones in Sicily.

There was only one truck there loaded with equipment. We knew that as soon as we blew it, other troops would be heading back to see what was going on. So, after blowing it, we cut the telephone lines and set up an ambush in a wooded area on the road coming in. It wasn't long before we heard vehicles coming, but they stopped, and we could see troops coming in on foot on the road. That's when we ambushed them, and we took no prisoners. We checked them off to make sure they were all dead.

Within an hour, we heard another patrol coming in and we ambushed them a bit further up the road. Again, we took no prisoners. There were about 25 men in each of those patrols.

After we had taken care of both patrols, we started moving to join the other American troops who were fighting their way up the boot. Somewhere not too far from the Bay of Salerno, the Navy brought in LSTs to pick us up and we and the other troops were taken by water around the mountainous terrain there, and we landed south of Naples at Maiori, a small town on the coast.

The Germans were in retreat. We had a few encounters with them, but not much opposition, and we were the first American troops into Naples. Mostly, especially later on, it was air raids we encountered. But they had left a bomb in a post office in Naples and it exploded a few days after we got there and killed a number of the 82nd boys and some civilians who were in the building.

We went on through Naples up to Anzio and stayed there a couple of days. Then we — the 505th Regiment — went back to Naples while the 504th stayed in Anzio.

We were in Italy about two months — September and October of 1943. While we were in Naples, we were staying in a bombed-out building — it was an old theater — just a couple of blocks from Garibaldi Square. Slick, being an Italian boy, became friends with a man and woman who operated a hotel right around the corner from Garibaldi Square, and that couple invited some of us to come over a couple of times.

So, me and Slick and Jake went over to where they stayed on the third floor of the hotel, and they served us wine and grape juice. I drank grape juice and they all drank wine. The room where we were drinking had big windows facing the street below and there was a little balcony outside the windows. Well, Jake got to feeling pretty good and cocky and said to Slick, "I'll bet you $5 that I can fly out that window and come back in."

Slick put his $5 on the table. And Jake went flying out one of those open windows over the balcony, just like a bird — three stories up — and landed on the cobblestone street below. He got up, walked back up the stairs, and collected his $5.

Two or three days later, we were doing the same thing again, and durn if he didn't go out that window again. Three stories up! You wouldn't believe it, but I saw it twice. But this time he broke his wrist. I knew he was tough, but he was nuts, too! He just flew out that window and landed on that cobblestone street. He was a character.

It was obvious that we were all ready for a rest, and in November our outfit was sent to England.

Chapter Six - Regrouping in England

On our way to England from Italy, we passed through Scotland and on to Ireland, where we stayed for about a month or so, somewhere near Belfast. It was in Belfast that I had my favorite picture of myself taken. Other than that, I didn't do much in Ireland. A couple of us would go into Belfast occasionally for a night or two, and go to a dance hall, but that was about it. We didn't have a chance to do a lot of cavorting — maybe some did, but we didn't. We were just recuperating from what we'd gone through in Sicily and Italy.

When we left Ireland, we were sent to Quorn, England, about 10 or 12 miles from Leicester. While we were there, we got acclimated to the damp climate and didn't do much of anything but exercising and marching. It was nothing to go on a 20-mile hike. Other than that, we made one practice jump. That night we stayed at the airstrip and it snowed about an inch or two. We didn't care about that as long as the weather was decent, so we went ahead and jumped.

I was coming down from about 1200 feet and I saw what I thought was a road below. Well, landing on a road doesn't hurt when you hit and roll, so I aimed for it and hit my target — and I went crashing through ice, because the "road" was a creek!

Fortunately, it wasn't deep, but I went in up to my waist. The other fellows got tickled at me. I was wet and it was cold, but that was sort of funny. And that was the only practice jump we made while we were there. While we were in England, the Allies were building up the troops and supplies for the invasion of Normandy, but, of course, they weren't telling us about it.

I couldn't tell Edna Lee much of anything about what I'd been doing either. We were writing each other, but my outfit moved around so much, it was hard to get the mail. It might be a month before I'd get a letter or two or three, when they'd catch up with me. I couldn't say much in my own letters except to ask about the family or tell a little bit about my friends in the outfit or their families, or to say something about the weather. Anything else and they (Army censors) would black it out.

I never had time to get homesick, though. Didn't have time to sightsee either — maybe some of the fellows did after the war was over, but I wasn't there when that happened.

I did get a chance to go into Leicester, however, when we weren't training. They had a real nice dance hall there and most of us liked to dance. Of course, a lot of them drank, but I didn't. I had learned my lesson about drinking when the outfit had first gotten overseas, several days after we had arrived in North Africa.

Before the 82nd had left Ft. Bragg, I had been playing on one of the baseball teams there and we had won the post championship and the team members were given 3-day passes. But before we could use the passes, we were sent to North Africa. So, after a few days overseas, they allowed us to use our passes and one of the fellows bought some local booze. I took two or three swallows of that stuff and vomited green for two days. I thought I was going to die. But I learned my lesson. So, in England I was drinking juice or lemonade or soda pop or something else when the others were drinking booze.

I wasn't a runabout either. I was always nice to the women, but so many of the men, of course, were there to see what they could get. It didn't bother me though. I didn't fool with them.

Mostly, we just waited around for five months, not really knowing exactly what we were preparing for. In the meantime, the eight men we had lost from our 30-man hit squad were replaced with some of the other fellows who had originally trained with us at Camp Claiborne.

Just before summer arrived in England, we found out we were going to be part of the invasion of Normandy.

But I didn't really envision what it was all about until I saw the vast armada of ships and boats in the English Channel as we were flying over them — on our way to war again on the night of June 5, 1944.

Chapter Seven — Fighting in France

My 30-man hit squad left England about 9:30 on the night of June 5, 1944. The remaining troops of the 82nd Airborne would follow us several hours later and the main Allied force would hit the beaches of Normandy the morning of June 6.

Our small team had a big job. Our objective was to destroy a communications unit located between the towns of Neuville and Ste. Mère Eglise. Reconnaissance plane photos had shown a mobile installation set up there in a wooded area of small trees. That unit apparently controlled German communications along the whole west coast of Europe from France to Norway.

Other than my landing on a rural outhouse when we hit our drop zone, this operation could not have gone more smoothly. Once we were all assembled on the ground, we moved without any contact to where the communications unit was sitting among the trees, and we surrounded that entire wooded area. It was just outside of Neuville and located right next to a road leading all the way to the Cherbourg peninsula. Amazingly, there were only two sentries guarding the communications site and they were slowly, nonchalantly walking around the compound, which had no gates and little camouflage.

Six of us in our three-man teams took care of them, no problem, no problem at all.

We then went to the door of the communications station, which was a lot like a mobile home. It was on wheels so that it could be pulled

81

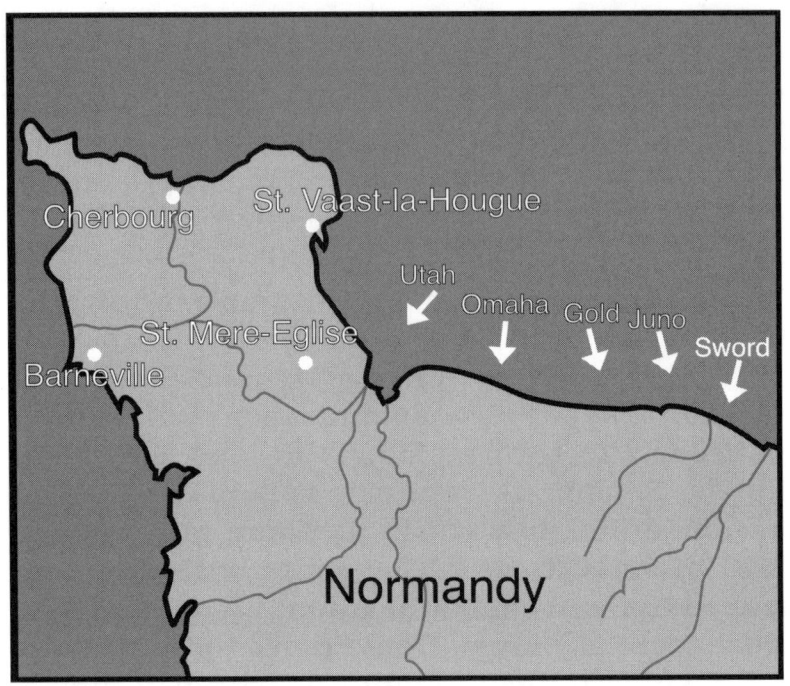

This map of Normandy shows where I was during the 33 days the 82nd Airborne fought in the Invasion of Normandy.

---

by another vehicle. We yanked open the door and four of us pitched grenades in simultaneously before slamming the door shut. We had to do that because we didn't want to give anyone time to give a signal or communicate anything, and we didn't want anyone to come out alive.

After it blew, we went in quick and there were four men inside, all dead. The interior was blown to pieces, too. The entire operation had been completed within about a half-hour of our 10:00 landing.

We immediately left and began working our way back up the highway, going along it until we got to the main artery going to Ste. Mère Eglise, about five miles away. We didn't encounter any action until we got there and about 4:30 that morning we joined the 3rd Battalion and began the liberation of Ste. Mère Eglise — the first town in France to be liberated.

Our luck as a behind-the-lines hit squad had always been good and we still had not lost a man on any of our special missions. We worked like machines, clocklike.

It was only when we rejoined our fellow troops that we'd lost men in Sicily, and that held true in France, too. At Ste. Mère Eglise, we lost 10 men from our 30-man squad, one of whom died in my arms. A German had ripped him apart with one of those machine pistols they used. Those burp pistols were twice as fast as our weapons, so you had to get the drop on them.

The Germans had flooded a lot of the low-lying areas around Ste. Mère Eglise so that we couldn't get across the Merderet River except by the bridges. When we tried to cross those, they'd let us have it, and about the only way we solved that was with the help of our air forces. They helped us a tremendous number of times.

The paratroopers who had jumped in at Ste. Mère Eglise had encountered all kinds of problems, too. They had come down in trees, on wires, and on rooftops. One fellow had landed on a church steeple. His name was John Steele and his plight was later portrayed in the movies. He was from Wilmington, North Carolina, and he was in my regiment, the 505th, but I didn't know him. I saw him before they cut him down — he was so high up, hanging there.

The Germans had shot at him when he got caught on the church steeple and I understand that they shot the heel off of his boot, but he had played dead and had survived.

The fighting was so intense that the first three days we were there, I didn't eat. The Germans were shelling us and I was tense, keeping my eyes open. Every position or area we took, they shelled us with mortars or artillery, and you could hear them coming in continuously.

On the third day, I got over in a ditch and looked out over the field in front of me and it looked like an Easter Egg hunt almost. Shells were lying all over the place, undetonated. I couldn't figure that out. I later was told that the Germans had been using Polish prisoners of war in their ammunition factories and those prisoners had found a way to fight back silently. They apparently had not put detonators in every fourth shell, and that's why so many of those shells had not exploded. They probably saved my life. I had some come within eight or 10 feet of me and not explode. I'd wait for them to go off and they'd just lay there with a little popping sound!

Anyhow, after I crawled into that ditch, I took my helmet off for just a minute — I didn't dare leave it off long. I looked at it and there were scratches all over it from little pieces of shrapnel that had hit it, which I hadn't even felt. Then I took my backpack off and when I looked at it, I saw two big holes in the back of it. I reached in and pulled out three cans of rations and all three cans had been cut in half by two pieces of shrapnel about the size of a quarter. The two pieces were lying in the bottom of the pack and if they had gone through me, they would probably have made a hole as big as a baseball. I never even felt them hit my pack!

Even though I hadn't eaten for three days, we never really hurt for anything to eat when in combat. We carried rations with us and we ate off the land if we had to. When we were away from supplies from headquarters, we had fellows in our group who had experience as cooks and butchers. They could butcher a pig or a calf or a chicken in no time flat. There were so many displaced animals with the shelling, and with people leaving their homes, they couldn't look after their livestock. But, we never took anything from anyone's home, at least our little group didn't. I guess some American troops did, but we didn't.

Like I said, we never worried too much about eating, and we could always find water, too. We had canteens and there were houses and wells in town, so there was no problem there.

Late one afternoon, just about dark, I heard shells coming in and I leaped into a ditch and landed on a woman and a baby. They had come out from Ste. Mère Eglise because of the shelling and, of course, she began crying and hollering when I landed on them. I had scared her almost to death — and it scared me for a second there, too. I hadn't known she was there and I hit right on top of her and her small baby.

I tried to calm her down, but I couldn't speak French, so I called over one of the boys who could and told him, "You stay with her until we get some help." He did and he got her to the medics. She wasn't wounded or anything, just scared. I don't think the baby was hurt either and I don't even remember it crying, although it probably did.

It's a horrible thing to see people losing everything they have or losing their lives. But that's war, I guess. I didn't actually see too many civilian casualties, but I think there were a lot up in Holland.

We stayed in Ste. Mère Eglise three or four days, waiting for the troops to come in from the beaches. We weren't that far from the coast, but they were having a lot of difficulty getting in from the beach.

The 82nd was about the first of the Allied troops to get together and we met up with the 101st Airborne and also with the British and Canadian troops, as well as with some Polish troops. We were all wearing an Allied patch on our sleeves at Normandy, and we wore them from then on. The Americans also had an American flag patch on the other sleeve.

After the others had joined us, each outfit spread out and we swung up to Cherbourg — actually, over to Barneville, then to Cherbourg to cut off that peninsula. There were about five divisions of Germans in that area and our objective was to take care of them, and that's what we did. From the time we landed in France, it took us 33 days of fighting without letup to do the job so that other troops could then take over.

That's how we operated. The 82nd would go in and take an area and then other troops, infantry, would come in and take over. Then we'd move out and start over. We spearheaded and that's why we lost so many men. Of the 11,770 men of the 82nd Airborne Division that went into

Normandy by parachute, glider, and landing craft, only 5,429 men made the return trip to England after the 33 days of fighting. It was after Normandy that our beloved leader Gavin — by now a Brigadier General — was given command of the entire 82nd Airborne. He was always in the thick of it with us.

It was on the 32nd day of our time in Normandy that I got hit for the second time in combat. I was checking the .30-caliber machine gun positions in our headquarters company's defensive position at St. Vaast-la-hougue, close to Cherbourg, when a sniper got me in the right calf, the same place I had been hit previously. It didn't really hurt, just stung.

It had to be a sniper because we didn't see anybody.

I was in France only one more day and then the whole 82nd went back to the coast where we were picked up to be taken back across the channel to England. As we were boarding the ship, I remember turning around to look at my runner, Slick, the dark-haired Italian boy, and his hair had turned white overnight. I had never seen anything like that. He had been scared to death. When we got to England, they put him in the hospital and we never did see him again. I don't know whether he lived or died.

Sometimes now I wonder how I kept going, seeing so much happen. It's hard to explain. You see it and you don't. You know it's happening, but you can't do much about it — just grit your teeth and go on. I guess I never really gave it much thought about it happening to me. With all the bullets and shrapnel flying around, you're just lucky if you don't get hit.

When we got back in England and checked in our equipment, it was like a morgue for three or four days. Nobody hardly spoke a word. Everybody was sort of walking around like a bunch of zombies. There were so many that didn't come back and we missed them, even though we hadn't really had a chance to get really attached to too many of them. We'd all been brought together so quick and, like I've said, we trained together for a few months and then the next thing we knew, we were in combat together.

Anyway, after three or four days, we began going back into Leicester again to the dance halls and beer halls and all. I enjoyed talking to some of the locals there and to some of the girls and that's just the way it was.

We knew it probably wouldn't be long before we were going back to fight the Germans again.

Chapter Eight — Fighting from Holland to Germany

We spent almost two months recuperating in England before we found ourselves making our first-ever daytime combat jump about 1:30 on the afternoon of September 17, 1944. This time we were jumping as part of a 20,000-man air armada that filled the skies of Holland with planes — including gliders — and paratroopers for three hours that afternoon.

More than 50 years after this jump, I had the occasion to meet a fellow from Holland who was a 17-year-old youngster when we jumped into his country. He told me then, "that's the prettiest sight I ever saw in my life." And I imagine it was.

Anyhow, our 30-man hit squad had been given the assignment to clear the Germans out of the small community of Groesbeek, near Nijmegen. That's what we did, but there really weren't too many of them there. After landing and assembling, we went house to house and building to building rooting them out, getting some very welcome help from the locals.

The houses and buildings in Groesbeek were mostly two- and three-story structures and the people were on the rooftops or at their windows waving colored cloth to let us know if Germans were in the building. They used green and red pieces. If you saw red, you knew the Germans were there. Green, of course, meant the building was clear.

Their signals helped a lot because search-

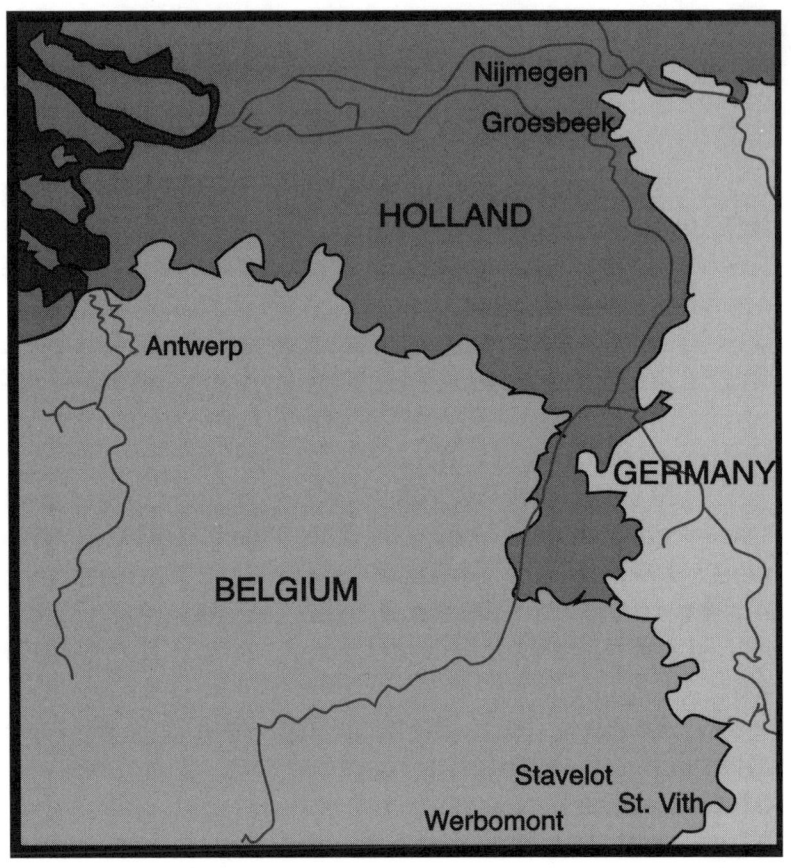

This map shows where I was in Holland and Belgium

ing those places, you were liable to get your head blowed off.

After we had accomplished our mission there, we headed to Nijmegen to help the rest of the 82nd Airborne clear that city of Germans. There we encountered more of the same, fighting Germans from building to building. Even with the help that the locals gave us with their signal cloths, we lost five more men from our original squad in the house to house fighting at Groesbeek and Nijmegen. This was the first time we'd lost any of our men when we were operating on our own, but it was so dangerous going building to building and being out in the open so much. During three days of fighting in Nijmegen, the 82nd held off six major counterattacks.

One of our major objectives in Nijmegen was to take the bridges which spanned the Waal River without allowing the Germans to blow them up. These bridges were enormous, the largest in Europe at that time. One was a mile and a half long and the Germans had rigged it with explosives. Our hit squad helped remove the explosives from it before they could be detonated. The Germans were apparently going to set them off from the post office in Nijmegen but somebody got to them first. We used that bridge to get our troops and tanks across, then we dug in and were there for about nine weeks in a stalemate.

It was during this stalemate that I lost my friend, Jake, who was our only remaining runner. We were being shelled one day and a shell landed right in his foxhole. We couldn't even find his dogtags.

By the time we left there to go to a rest area in Sissone, France, we had lost six men from our hit squad during the fighting in Holland. There were now only six of us left of our original 30-man unit, and the 82nd had suffered almost 3,000 wounded in Holland.

We hadn't been at Sissone long when the Battle of the Bulge in Belgium broke out on December 16. This was Adolf Hitler's last stand — a counteroffensive involving 250,000 German soldiers who were trying to take back Antwerp, Belgium. Our diminished hit squad was given enough new guys to get us back to 30 and we were then sent to St. Vith, not too far from Stavelot in Belgium. We arrived there about 2:30 on the morning of December 18. St. Vith was being surrounded by the Germans, including the 1st SS Panzer division, and our job was to stop them and prevent them from overrunning our troops and getting to Antwerp.

They gave each of us a bazooka and sent 15 of us to one position and 15 to another point at road junctions. For the next four days — in deep snow, heavy fog, and bitter cold to 10 below zero — we held those positions so that the remnants of four American divisions could pull back. It was so cold, we had to keep moving to avoid freezing. On the fourth day, the fog began to lift and our Allied pilots came in and really laid it on their armored vehicles and munitions.

The Panzer division that was there was the same one that had massacred about 100 captured 82nd Airborne troops — lined them up in front of their tanks and mowed them down with their machine guns — at Malmedy. Our 504th regiment caught up with those SS troops during the Battle of the Bulge and completely wiped them out.

After our bombers had done their work, the fighting let up somewhat. Within a month, our troops were moving to attack the Siegfried line in Germany, with the 82nd being the first to breach it in the first week of February 1945. This was all done in deep snow and bitter cold conditions.

Moving into the Siegfried line, I had one of my hardest experiences during the war. We had just gotten a replacement in our unit, a boy about 18 years old. He had been on the front line with us for about two hours when the Germans began to shell us and he and I were making our way to a machine gun bunker. He was about 10 yards behind me when I heard a shell explode back there. He hollered and I turned around and he was lying on the ground. Both of his legs were gone. I got on the ground with him real quick. He was in deep shock and I held him as tight as I could.

By the time the medics got to us, there was blood all over both of us, and he was dead in my arms. They had to pry my arms open as they took him and I just got up, walked over behind a large tree, sat down, and cried. I still have flashbacks about that and it still hurts.

Once we were through the Siegfried line, the weather started letting up and it became mostly a mop-up operation for us. We still had some more to go but, for the most part, we only met small pockets of resistance. During this fighting in Germany, we lost two more men from our original team of 30.

We had made it to a little town not far from Cologne near the end of February when General Gavin sent for me, Arnie, Bob and Gary — the four acting sergeants — the only men left from the original 30-man squad. All of us had been wounded two or three times since we had seen our first combat in Sicily, a long year and a half earlier. We had been in and out of combat for 371 days and we were worn out. We looked like Sad Sacks.

During the war, the Armed Forces gave you points for time in combat and time overseas and when you accumulated enough, you could be sent home. All four of us had more than enough points to have been sent home long ago, but we had stuck it out. Gavin knew that and when he called us together then, he congratulated us, saluted us, and then surprised us by hugging our necks — a general! And he told us that he was sending us to Paris where we would be checked out medically — physically and mentally — and then we would be sent home, while the rest of the 82nd was being sent back to Sissone for another rest period!

I was ready. I had been sick for the last several weeks, vomiting and suffering diarrhea — and that's rough in cold weather. I didn't know what was wrong with me, just thought I had a bad upset stomach. Once I got to Paris, however, I found out. I had an ulcer — and that's what I ended up getting a discharge on! Not my wounds, but an ulcer. I was the only one of the four of us that got a medical discharge and it was for an ulcer.

Nowadays they say that ulcers are caused by bacteria, so somewhere along the line I guess I drank some bad water with bacteria in it. Or maybe it was from the snow and ice — I'd eat a little bit of snow, too. I don't know.

Anyway, after spending two weeks getting checked out in a hospital in Paris, they put us all on a plane heading home. I remember we were waiting there in the terminal and I had a carton of cigarettes under my arm — they gave us all cigarettes every week. I guess about 90% of the fellows smoked — nervous energy. I always traded mine, of course, ever since we'd started getting

This is how I looked shortly before I was discharged in 1945.

them in North Africa. There I had traded mine to the Arabs for eggs and fruit — and for a pack of Camels with that picture of the camel on it, I could get three times as much as I could with any other brand.

Anyhow, I was standing there in the Paris airport with those cigarettes when a fellow walked up to me and said, "Let me sell that carton of cigarettes for you." I said, "Okay."

He wasn't gone but two or three minutes before he came back and gave me $20. That was big money! I don't know what he got for them — maybe $40 or $50 — but I didn't care. I was headed home with money in my pocket.

Chapter Nine — Coming home and going on

When we left France, our first stop was the Azores where we refueled on a small island. I've never seen so much wind blow as they had there. The pilot had to make three passes at the field before he could land, the wind was so strong. That was only the second time I had ever landed in a plane and I didn't know if we were going to make it!

Then when we got out of the plane to go to the PX there, we had to hold hands or the wind would've blown us down!

When we left the Azores, we had a little engine trouble out over the Atlantic before we landed in Newfoundland. They gave us another plane there. I'm glad that we flew at night most of the time. I didn't have to look at that ocean. I don't know how they ever find people out in the ocean — you can't see anything but water. Nothing!

Anyway, we finally made it across the ocean and landed at La Guardia in New York City. When we got out of the plane, Arnie, Bob, Gary and I grabbed each other by the hand, and went to the rear of the plane where we all kissed the tail of that big transport. Then we got down on our knees and kissed the ground, all four of us. Then we said a little prayer.

As soon as I could, I called Edna Lee to let her know I would soon be home. She was working for the telephone company in Huntington and was the long distance operator and when I called, we didn't recognize each other's voices. She passed me through to her mother's house!

When I spoke to her mother, she said, "Well, I'm sorry, but she's at work." So she got me connected back to her and Lee liked to have had a fit. The phone company let her off work right then and she went home, even though I told her I'd call her in a couple of days as soon as I knew when and where I would be going.

They kept us in another hospital there for a couple of days and then they sent each of us to the discharge camp nearest our homes. I was sent to Camp Butler outside of Durham and Lee got there the next day. It was the first time we had seen each other in almost two years, and only the third time we'd ever been together and I was a little anxious sitting there on the bench when her bus came in. I didn't know if she would recognize me or if I would recognize her. But it was fine.

She stayed with me for two or three days and then went on to Greensboro to stay with my parents since I had to stay in the hospital until I got my discharge. On March 19, 1945, I received my discharge and I left for Greensboro to be with Lee.

We stayed with my parents for three or four months and I got a temporary job with the recreation department in Greensboro. Then the community out at Pomona Mills called my old coach, Bob Jamieson, about starting a summer recreation program for their area. He told them that he didn't have time to do it because he was so involved with Greensboro High School and the swimming team, but he knew someone who might be available and willing. He recommended me.

So I went out to Pomona Mills and they hired me for the summer. I got a program going for the youngsters there — baseball for the boys and softball for the girls, plus basketball, bowling, and a few other activities. We only had 9 boys — ages 14 and 15 — on the baseball team but we had the city championship team that summer. One of our players was Lindy Brown, brother of Skinny Brown, who was a Major League baseball player. I, of course, had not finished my college degree because of being drafted, so when the summer program ended, I began college again, this time at Guilford College in Greensboro.

I didn't want to return to N. C. State College because it was a technical school and I wasn't interested in any of that. While at Guilford in 1945, I helped Doc Newton with the football team there. I didn't play, just acted as the backfield coach while I took a few courses. Then basketball season rolled around and he didn't want to coach basketball, so he asked me if I would. I wasn't a basketball player and never played it in high school, but I took it on.

The following year, 1946, I helped the coach recruit a bunch of football players, including a half-dozen that had played at N.C. State. We also had one that had played at Carolina, one from Villanova, one from Catawba, two from Elon College — and me. We had a slew of older ex-ball players, and most all of them had been in the service. One was my friend Robert (Lody) Glenn, who had been my teammate at Greensboro High School. Lody had been a major in the Marines during the war and later became a teacher, coach, and principal at Greensboro High School.

He and I became co-captains of the Guilford college football team in 1946. We had a pretty good little team there for about five or six games, but then we started getting hurt and lost two or three games at the end of the season. We still ended up with a pretty good record though.

About that time, the principal at Liberty High School, Don Keesler, was looking for someone to coach their sports teams. Lee was working at Coble Sporting Goods down on Greene Street, doing all the engraving and paperwork and other things for them, and he came asking there. They told him about me and, even though I had not gotten my degree yet, they let me take a provisional certificate and I got the job.

For the next two years, 1947 and 1948, I

The 1947-48 Liberty High School football team which I was proud to coach. That's me in the white T-shirt.

My beautiful wife, Edna Lee Kearns Dickerson, as she looked in the 1950s.

---

coached the teams at Liberty High School. Lee and I had bought a little 5-room house in Greensboro at 1128 W. Northwood Street in 1945, after we left my parents home, so we switched houses with a fellow from Liberty who worked in Greensboro, and for the next two years we lived in his house in Liberty. It worked out fine.

Lee had gone to summer school at Woman's College (now the University of North Carolina at Greensboro) and she was real good at shorthand and typing. She was an honor student throughout all her school years — grammar, high school, and in summer school. After a few months at Woman's College, her instructors wanted her to go ahead and take the exams, and she took them early and passed all the courses! So while we were in Liberty, she taught typing and shorthand.

While I was coaching in Liberty we had some pretty good ball clubs there. I also coached the American Legion baseball team one summer and Howard Coble — now a Congressman for North Carolina — played first base for us. He was only about 17 then, and he'll tell you now that he couldn't hit a lick. I still tease him about it.

Since I wanted to continue being a school coach, I had to get my degree, so at the end of 1948, I went over to High Point College to finish up, since Guilford College didn't have a degree program in phys ed/social studies. Back in those days you had to be a teacher in order to be a coach, so I got my teacher's certificate at High Point College in 1949.

While I was at High Point, the coach, Ralph James, also wanted me to help him with their football team, which I did. Lee had begun working at Coble's Sporting Goods again, and I was still drawing GI Bill money, so we were making it, just fair.

During the last year I played football in college, the coach asked me if I'd like to go up and work out with the Redskins to see if I could play pro ball. I just laughed and said, "Coach, I appreciate you asking me, but I want to live just a little bit longer. Thank you."

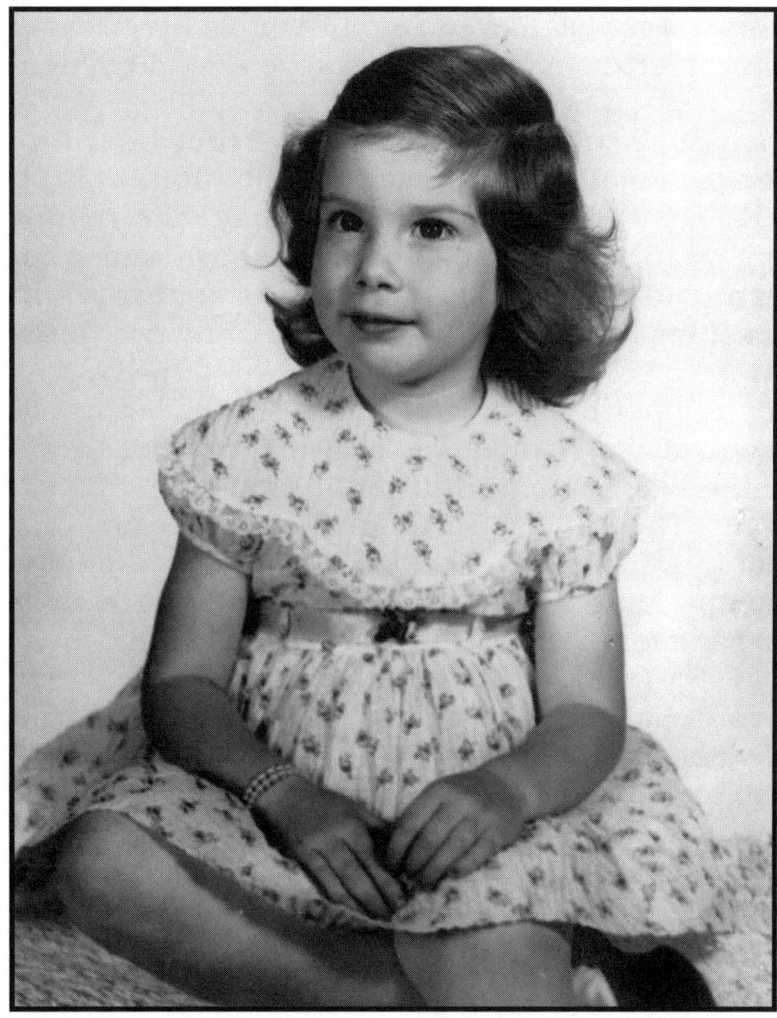

Becky as she looked in May 1954. She was 3 1/2 years old.

My brother Herman had played pro ball, of course, and he'd told me it was rough. I wasn't big enough and I probably wouldn't have lasted the first day.

When I left High Point College, I went to Gibsonville High School and coached there for a year. We rented our house in Greensboro to a couple that year, even as our own family became three instead of two. That was the year our daughter Becky was born, December 6, 1950.

She was and still is a beautiful kid. She was so small and looked so fragile that, at first, I didn't want to hold her! Anyway, the following year we returned to Greensboro and I began looking for other work. Coaching and teaching didn't pay a whole lot. For two years I worked for my uncle, Hunter Welker, who was my mother's brother. He was a contractor and I just did odd jobs, roofing and a bit of everything else, helping him build houses.

Then in 1952 I took the Postal exam and got on with them. They paid pretty good money compared to what a lot of other folks were making and for the next 29 years, until my retirement in 1980, I stayed with them. I was never that crazy about the Postal Service but it was a job that paid decent and I wasn't going to flit around from one job to another.

I worked at what they called the RPO — the Railroad Post Office. We had a terminal next to the depot downtown on Washington Street and we worked the mail out of there for the whole state. Truckloads of mail would be brought in and we would sort it out and put it on the postal cars. A lot of it was mail from the Sears mail order house in Greensboro, although we also handled a lot of letters. I mostly worked in what they called the three CPX — circulars, papers, and small parcels. Sometimes I would move to first class mail and I learned to handle registered mail.

In those days, a lot of the mail was worked even after it was put on the trains and sometimes I would go out at night on the postal trains and sort the mail from Greensboro to Goldsboro, or to North Wilkesboro, Charlotte, or some other place like Charlottesville, Virginia. I usually worked in the terminal and substituted on the trains.

Then, in the 60s, they took the postal cars off the trains and used buses going into the smaller towns. Trains couldn't do what the buses could, stop at the small towns all over the state. In 1966, however, they ended that and built the post office down on East Market Street where I stayed until my retirement. When I retired, I was given credit for 32 years — my three years of military service plus 29 years of postal service.

While I was working for the Postal Service, I continued to coach for a number of years. I coached Burtner American Legion baseball for a couple of years, both at Liberty and in Greensboro. Then a good friend of mine, Bill Feeney, asked me if I would start a football and basketball program at Notre Dame High School, a Catholic school that no longer exists, but which was located on Summit Avenue at old St. Leo's Hospital.

I said, "Sure. I'll be glad to."

So, for four years, 1959 through 1962, I did

that. I got paid very little, just enough for gas, but I enjoyed it. Discipline wasn't any problem in those days, and when you have that, everything works out fine. It's so much different now than then.

I was also doing a lot of volunteer coaching during all these years, Little League baseball teams, Midget football teams, and American Legion teams. I did not get anything for it, but I enjoyed doing it.

Anyhow, while I was at Notre Dame High School, we had some pretty good ball players. Al McGuire — who coached at Belmont Abbey then and later led Marquette University to the NCAA basketball championship — had one of my boys play for him at Belmont. His name was Roy King, and I got a nice letter from Al talking about how good Roy was. Another student, Pat Moriarty ended up at Virginia Tech. So, for a little school — we didn't have but about 125 students — we had some good little ball clubs, both football and basketball.

Back then it was hard for us to get ball games, too. We were integrated and other schools wouldn't play you if you had a colored boy on your ball club, and I had a couple. We played Bessemer a couple of times — the jayvee team, because the varsities wouldn't play us. That was just the way it was. Those other schools didn't have integration then, 1960 to 1962.

We could play the other Catholic schools, however — Gibbons in Raleigh, McGuiness in Winston-Salem, and Charlotte Catholic in Charlotte. We also played the Lynchburg and Roanoke Catholic schools in Virginia.

After 1962, however, I didn't do any more coaching. I missed it, but not the classroom teaching part. I wasn't that enthused about being a teacher, but I had to be that to be a coach. I had to teach social studies and civics and history classes and phys ed, in addition to coaching.

I enjoyed the coaching, watching young fellows grow and become young men, teaching discipline, and motivating them to do the best they could with what they had, mentally and physically. Coaches had to do a lot more back then than just coach, though. I would help line off the field and take in towels and wash them myself — take 'em home and wash them. I'd let the boys take their uniforms home at times, too, their practice stuff, and wash it and bring it back. We just didn't have the equipment and facilities back then that you have now and, on top of that, the schools didn't pay you much.

But I have a lot of fond coaching memories. I think one of the best is when I was coaching at Notre Dame High School. We were going to play Roanoke Catholic and the week before we played them, Lee and I went up to scout them in Alta Vista, Virginia. They were a large school and we had only about 20 players on our squad. Alta Vista was also a big, bruising club but they just barely beat Roanoke by one point and I thought, "Oh, Lord."

Lee usually came to our games but the next week when we went to play them, I told her, "you just stay home tonight." We weren't supposed to win but when I returned home that morning about 1 or 2 o'clock I woke her up and said, "You know what? We won!" We had won 7-0 on a pass play and I was just shocked that we had been able to beat them because they really had a better ball club than us. I played in a lot of high school and college football games, but I guess that was the most memorable of all of them.

Anyway, after I was with the Postal Service for a number of years, I got out of coaching and picked up playing golf and fishing, and settled for that. I would go to the mountains with H.G. Johnson, a friend of mine from the Post Office. We worked together for almost 30 years.

His wife was from West Jefferson, North Carolina, so we would go trout fishing up there and also in West Virginia. It was right much fun. I wasn't very good at fly fishing, so I used a spin caster. Just used corn and worms for bait — most of the time corn. Just put a little bitty weight on there and a piece of corn. Most times I didn't have any success, but I caught a few. Of course, it's not much fun until you fall in a few times, but that's part of it. The rocks are slippery!

While I was coaching, Lee always went to the ball games, but I don't think she ever cared much about playing any kind of sports. She and a girl friend used to play some tennis, but that's the only thing. She thought my golfing was silly.

I used to play my golf out at Bryan Park and down at Longview and Sandy Ridge. I wasn't that good a golfer, but I liked to play at least once a week and sometimes two times. Lord, I even got a trophy for one of our postal tournaments.

I also got a hole-in-one on a blind shot at the Monticello Golf Course. Used a 9-iron on a par 3 hole and didn't even see the ball go in the hole. We got down there and walked around and looked everywhere and I finally walked over on the green and looked down in the hole and there it was. So I hollered at the other fellows before I touched it so I'd be sure that they saw it!

When Becky got old enough, we'd play a little golf together, too, at Longview or Cedar Crest or Monticello — small courses. I'd get irritated a lot of the times, however, because she had long hair. I'd try to get her to put it up in a bun while she was on the course and she wouldn't. She'd stand up there and flip that hair back, and I'd say, "Becky, put your hair up so you can hit the ball!"

I am not too patient. When I want something done, I do it. No pussy-footing around. You've seen people that piddle? Well, fellows that are used to doing something and just go on and do it, when we see somebody else not doing it, we think they should. Of course, I know folks are different...but still...

Becky and I were real close and we still are. We get together every week for lunch. She's married now to William C. Whitlock, III — Bill — and they have two teenage sons, Brian and Stephen.

When Becky was little, we played together all the time — little games and sports and such. I would take her to her dancing lessons and we played tennis, as well as golf. She started the tennis when she was 7 or 8. I would take her to see movies like Snow White and Bambi, too.

Becky also liked to go fishing when she was little — she liked catching little ole crappies, so I would take her to Lake Brandt. I don't think she has time to fish now though.

Becky when she was a senior at Page High School in 1969.

She was just one of those kids that never caused any trouble. I think I spanked her just one time — and it really wasn't a spanking. She was kind of smart talking me once — I was tell-

Becky and me in 1997. She's a nurse (RN) now and a mother of two boys, Brian and Stephen, and still a beautiful "kid" to me.

---

ing her to do something and she wouldn't do it. I chased her around the house and found her hiding behind the bed.

Another time she came home from school and told me that the teacher had spanked her. Well, I didn't much think so, but I told her I'd go see. So, I went over to Irving Park and the teacher laughed and said, "Oh, we were coming back from the auditorium and there were some stragglers and I went back there and gave them a push — and she thought I spanked her!"

She was just a good girl.

Lee was a good girl, too. We got along great. People don't believe me when I tell them that in 54 years of marriage, we never had an argument, not so you could tell it. Nobody believes it, but it's true.

She worked most of the time we were married, and she did all the cooking — I'm no cook. She did most of the housework, but I helped some. She also did all of the inside painting, which I despise doing. She'd paint anything that would stand still. I bet she painted the refrigerator a half-dozen times. Of course, I did all the outside work. And we both looked after Becky — I looked after her as much as Lee did.

Lee was a little feisty and she had a temper, but she never did show it too much to me. She was a lot like me, but a little bit more of a go-getter. She didn't pussy-foot around when she wanted to do something. She didn't make no bones about it — if she wanted something done, she wanted it done. Got a little irritated if you didn't do it.

She was good at doing most anything she wanted to do. She was one of the best dancers in the state of West Virginia before we married, and for a time she danced on a river boat, the *Island Queen*, that traveled up and down the Ohio River. She was also real good at swimming, and that's one reason we eventually got a swimming pool for our backyard.

The other reason we got the pool is that we went to the beach one time — and I've never been too crazy about the beach — to a cottage at Wendy Hill. We were going to stay for a week but it rained all day long for the first three days and I said, "Let's go home." So we packed up and when we got back home I said, "I'm going to build a swimming pool."

That was 21 years ago and after that, both

Lee and I swam about every day we could in the spring and summer — and I still do, about 25 or 30 laps every day. The pool is 16 by 36 feet.

Becky had graduated from high school around that time and I remember her saying to me, "How come you didn't build it before now!"

The truth was we didn't have much money to put out for expensive stuff like a pool before then. My dad had died around 1955 after receiving his first Social Security check, which we then had to turn around and send back. He had just turned 65 and died of a stroke. My mother was still working at a dry cleaners, taking in the dry cleaning and setting it out at the front counter. She continued doing that until she was close to 80, and she lived to be 92. But during the last 25 years of her life, Lee and I spent a lot of time looking after her. She was drawing about $156 a month in Social Security and didn't have enough to live on. So we found her a small four-room house at 513 S. Holden and I took care of it, the house and land. Then we had to put her in the nursing home at Evergreens and while she was there, she fell and broke her hip. After she got out of the hospital, we put her in a place at Starmount and that's where she died.

During those years, while Lee's parents were alive — her Dad died at 74 and her mother lived to be over 90 — we would go up to West Virginia for two or three days several times a year. But we couldn't stay too long since my mother was by herself.

Four years after mother died in 1986, Lee began to have health problems. She was bothered by her right knee and her right hip and she could hardly walk. She went to a neurosurgeon and he ended up operating on her spine — said it was a nerve. It didn't do any good though and she had two more back operations, one each year for three years.

She then had a bad ulcer. One night, about 1 o'clock or 1:30, she sat up and said she didn't know what was the matter with her. She couldn't lie down or turn right or left, so I said, "let me take you to the emergency room." No, she didn't want to go right then. She kept sitting there and sitting there, so I just got up and picked her up, put her in the car, and drove her to the emergency room. This was about 2 o'clock in the morning.

They put her on a table there and I wish you could have seen her — she looked like a balloon being blown up. I thought she was going to explode. What had happened was that during the night her ulcer had blown open a hole between her stomach and intestines and she was being poisoned by the liquids flowing in there.

They operated on her and she was in intensive care for seven days. She like to have died.

The next year, she had another back operation. Then she had several more again. None of them helped. She had six of them. Different doctors cut up on her. And then the ulcer again.

I took her to the hospital again but it wasn't the same thing. Then, while she was in Cone Hospital, she had a stroke. I'd gone to Sunday school that morning and came back to the hospital to see her, and one of the nurses just nonchalantly said, "Your wife had a stroke."

No doctor ever said a word to me or nothing. I didn't believe it.

She was paralyzed all on her left side. She was in the hospital for a pretty good while — I think they let you stay 22 days under Medicare — and then she got 22 more days of extended care. We were there for almost two months at $3000 a month. I couldn't stand it. I didn't have that kind of money and she wasn't getting better.

I'd go over and a lot of the time they hadn't even cleaned her by noon. And she smoked and they wouldn't let anyone smoke in the room. I'd have to pick her up myself a lot of the time and put her in her wheelchair and take her outside. I kept doing that, so I just brought her home.

Lee and me in the late 1980s, before her health problems began.

So after six back operations, two stomach operations, and a stroke, I had Lee at home for two years, doing everything I could for her in 1996 and 1997. I had different women coming in, too, but they often wouldn't show up or call — nothing. At first we got a little help working with physical therapy for her arm and leg, but it didn't do any good. The therapists tried and they did a good job because I was right there with them most of the time. They really tried, but just finally had to give up.

Lee could talk but she was paralyzed all

on the left side and she couldn't stand or do anything. I gave her about 12 or 13 medications twice a day and two shots of a muscle relaxant twice a day. She got cramps in her legs and couldn't stay in bed long. I'd move her anywhere from eight to 10 times every 24 hours. She weighed about 150 pounds and was as solid as a rock, and I wasn't all that young to be lifting — but I had a lifting belt and I knew how to do it. I'd put her in the chair and in bed. I did it all. Changed her, cleaned her. After dealing with the women who wouldn't show up, I did it myself, every bit of it.

Much of the time she'd sit in the lift chair in the back room near the pool. I had cleaned her up one day and taken her there and had then gone to another room to write some checks. I had the TV turned on for her and checked on her about every 15 minutes and she seemed to be okay. Then when I came in to check, she seemed to be looking at the ceiling, with her head back to the side. I thought she was looking at the ceiling fan, but when I tried to talk to her, she wouldn't answer. And about that time, Becky came in the door, looked at her, and said, "You'd better call an ambulance."

I called and sure enough, she'd had another stroke sitting right there. We got her to the hospital between 1 o'clock and 1:30 and they kept her in the emergency room and contacted her physician, Dr. Stafford. He called me to the phone and, having talked with the medical folks there, he told me, "It doesn't look good at all. I'll keep in touch with you from the emergency room where I am." And he did. Later, he called me back and said, "I'll be over about 5 o'clock and check her."

Becky was there with me and when Dr. Stafford looked Lee over, he just shook his head. She didn't know anybody, although when we had first got her there, she had seemed to, but had just gone downhill. They kept her there in the emergency room a little longer and then Dr. Stafford said, "take her on upstairs." She died on the way up.

So Lee had a very rough time for 7 or 8 years. After all those operations, she still had that pain, and the bills totaled around $350,000. I still owe between $75,000 and $80,000 myself. They told me, "you can pay two or three

This photograph was taken several years before Lee died. In front, left to right, are our grandsons, Stephen and Brian. Sitting with me and Lee are Becky and our son-in-law, Bill Whitlock. All of us are members of the West Market United Methodist Church in Greensboro. I have been a faithful member of the Fellowship Class there since 1962.

hundred dollars a month." That's what I'll have to do. I don't have that kind of money, though. I spent so much looking after my mother.

Everybody's got their problems, their troubles, and their expenses, I'm sure, so I've never asked for any help. Physically, mentally, I've always been able to do a lot of things.

I had never told Lee the things I'd done in the war until our last years together though. I didn't tell her a thing about what I'd done in the war for 50 years. Then, in 1995, on the 50th anniversary of the end of World War II, we were sitting out on the porch and I told her. She just shook her head in disbelief. There wasn't much she could say.

There are fewer and fewer of us who were there who are still left to say what happened there. I don't want people to forget — and I want our young people to know. So, not long after that conversation and before Lee's death, I created my mini-museum of World War II history and artifacts.

Chapter 10 — Honoring those who did their duty

Even before I told Lee what I did in the war, I found myself thinking more and more about the events that I had witnessed a half-century earlier, and feeling a need to share them. In the spring of 1995, I took my medals and other military mementos out of my trunk and showed them to my son-in-law, Bill Whitlock. He said, "Let me have those medals and I'll frame them for you," which he did.

Then I decided to cut some pictures out of an Airborne book I had and to take other information about World War II and paste all of those things on poster boards. On May 8, 1995 — 50 years after the surrender papers were signed in Europe — I put the poster boards on eight easels out in my driveway. I just displayed them in a staggered line, along with a sign inviting people to stop and look, and I was amazed at how neighbors and people driving by reacted when they saw the displays. They'd forgotten — or never knew — much about World War II, and they were interested and appreciative.

When Lee saw how much it meant to me to be able to share my experiences and the experiences of other World War II veterans, she said that I ought to start a little museum with all the stuff I had. So, that's what I did.

We had a 10-foot by 17-foot pool house in our backyard and I took all the pool supplies, boxes, exercise equipment, and other odds and ends out of it. I replaced all of that with photographs, newspaper articles and maps, various weapons, uniforms, and equipment, models of planes and ships, and other items and relics from the war. In addition to what I already had, other veterans donated a lot of things, and one of my neighbors — Frank Potts, a Vietnam veteran — helped me arrange the exhibits.

One wall had numerous items related to the Pacific theater, including a Japanese flag and sword, and parachute shrouds from a Japanese paratrooper. There was also a "Faces of the Enemy" exhibit with photos of General Tojo, Admiral Yamamoto, Tokyo Rose, and the Japanese officials who were at the surrender ceremony aboard the battleship Missouri.

On the opposite wall, I put artifacts of the European and North African campaigns. In addition to many items and photos commemorating our American fighting men, I included paraphernalia such as a small photo album I found on a dead German soldier and photos of Hitler, Field Marshall Rommel, and Propaganda Minister Goebbels — some of the men most responsible for the nightmarish European experiences of World War II.

I also had a table in the middle of the museum with other items — a canteen, gas mask, and so forth. Nearby, there were scale models of U.S., German, Russian, and Japanese airplanes, plus replicas of other military vessels and vehicles, including a PT boat and a Sherman tank.

On Saturday, March 2, 1996, I officially opened my WWII mini-museum to the public with free admission to all. I was honored to have Howard Coble — our Congressman and my friend since I coached him in youth baseball — cut the ribbon for the opening.

From opening day until June of 1998, when I donated most of the items in the museum to Greensboro's Historical Museum, thousands of people from 25 states and six foreign countries visited the museum and signed the guestbook.

Many other people and organizations pitched in to make the museum a success during this time. Dr. Fred Lupton donated a picnic table for visitors to sit at, as did Ed Kinard of Kinards Drug Store. The local K-Mart stores donated another picnic table for outside the museum, and stools for the interior. And many other individuals donated items they had for display.

My museum welcomed — at no charge — any and everyone from noon to 6 p.m., seven days a week, and was open for longer hours on holidays such as Veterans' Day and July the 4th. Many veterans came and expressed their appreciation for what I was doing to help others remember what they had done. One very special visitor was Barbara Gavin Fauntleroy, the daughter of General James M. Gavin, my former commander. In addition, I had the pleasure of doing presentations in many of the schools in and around Greensboro and of having other school groups and organizations (such as Scouts) tour the museum.

It was and is especially important for me to have our young people know about the sacrifices that those who preceded them made so that they can enjoy the freedoms they have. And it has been the responses of the youngsters that mean the most to me, especially the letters so many of them have written me after seeing the museum or hearing me talk about the war.

Those of us who were there can never forget, nor do we want others to forget. Even if we didn't want to remember, that's not possible — and it wouldn't be right.

Dear Mr. Dickerson, 12-1-97

I would like to tell you what a fabulous time I had at your museum. I came just today with my Girl Scout Troop. Not only I, But my whole troop was fascinated by what you had to tell us. It was so interesting that I just wanted to sit there and listen to your stories all day long! I really enjoyed hearing where you landed after jumping out of a plane. I can't believe you landed on an outhouse and a cow! I know that when you were in World War II you had many adventures, and you just couldn't fit them into your tour in this one day. Hopefully, and probably I will be back visiting you to hear about them. Again, I would like to thank you for the excellent tour and your magnificent museum.

 Sincerely,
 Anne Y. Upson   Anne Y. Upson
 (A member of Girl Scout Troop #986)

P.S. Thank you for the snacks. Also, thank you for the canned goods.

I received many letters from both adults and young people who visited my museum. This delightful example is from 12-year-old Anne Upson of Greensboro, NC.

The site of my World War II mini-museum – our former pool house behind our home at 1128 W. Northwood St., Greensboro, NC.

I am reminded of the war daily, not only through the flashbacks I've come to expect, but even through events that I don't expect. For example, I recently had a lower intestinal ailment and I went to the doctor. After he took x-rays, he asked me how long I'd had the bullet in me.

I said, "What bullet?"

He showed me my x-ray and, much to my surprise, there was a bullet lodged near my upper right leg bone. When I thought about it, I realized that it had to be the sniper's bullet that detonated the grenade on me in Sicily — I had carried it for half a century and not even known it was there! And it's still there, imbedded in me, as are the experiences I and others shared during those days not really so long ago.

Most of those men — and all of the men that served with me in our 30-man squad — are

One of the display walls inside my WWII museum. Thousands of adults and children visited and learned here in 1996, '97, and '98.

dead now. If they could still talk, they would have their own stories to tell, and could corroborate what I've said in this book. I am sure that whatever they had to say, they would want people to know and remember what they experienced and accomplished during the war.

I only saw Arnie and Bob one more time after the war and that was shortly after we had all been discharged. But I saw Gary not long before he died. He came through Greensboro in 1993 and stayed with me several days. When he got ready to leave, he told me that his doctors had told him he only had about six months to live. He had cancer. He went on to Florida and about two months later, I received a letter from a nurse telling me that he had died.

Before Gary left me though, he gave me the Airborne book that I used to cut pictures from for my museum. He told me when he gave me the book that I ought to share what was in it with others, especially kids, so they would know what we'd been through. And I've done that.

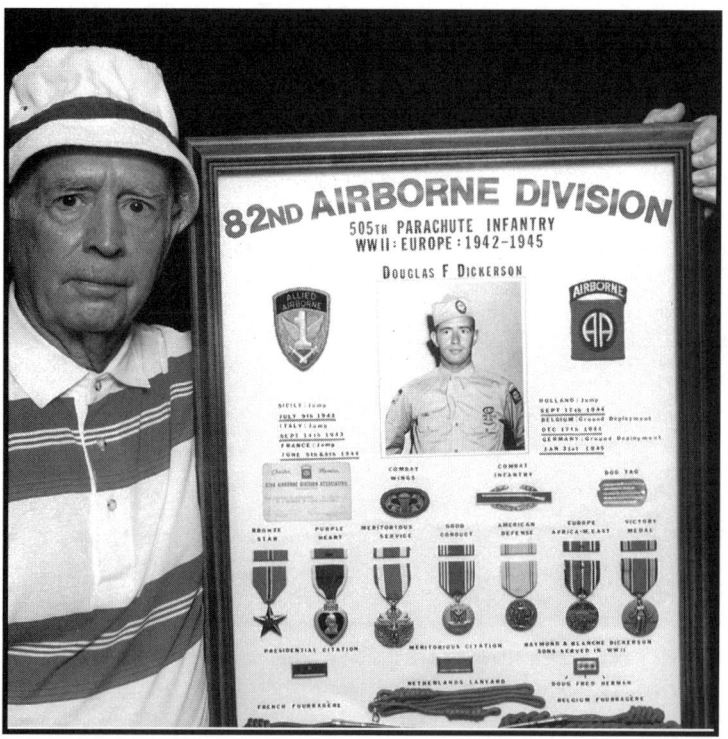

Here I am with a very personal display that was included as part of my World War II mini-museum. My son-in-law, Bill Whitlock, created the display for me.

Now I feel like I've done just about everything I could, and I'm hoping others will carry on and do the things that need to be done to keep our country and our world free.

To those who are conscientious objectors, I would say: no one wants war. But there comes a time when you have to be prepared for it. If you protest, but don't do anything about aggressors, they will run over you — as you complain, "why didn't someone do something about them?"

Do you understand how vicious dictators are — raping women and children, destroying people and property? To a dictator, you are noth-

My expression doesn't show it here, but I have enjoyed doing my part to help folks remember those who did their duty.

ing. I have seen it with my own eyes. Ask veterans from any war — Korea, Vietnam, Desert Storm.

Would you rather have war in your own country or help other countries stop the atrocities there before they happen here?

Before my fighting days ended in Europe, I had the sickening experience of seeing the extermination camps in Werbomont and Stavelot, where bodies were stacked on top of each other. I helped force German soldiers to bury those bodies. And I remember a German officer telling me that if we hadn't stopped them, they would have done away with all the Jews, Blacks, and "undesirables" — not only in Europe, but in Canada and the United States, too.

So, I will keep telling people that we need to go to these hotspots all over the world and put out the fires, or we'll have other dictators trying to take over the world. And instead of fighting them there, we'll be fighting them here on this continent. Would you rather fight them here or there?

Yes, a lot of innocent people die and are maimed for life in war, but many more will suffer those fates if we don't do away with the leaders and the staffs who cause the aggression. We must go straight to the source, wherever it is.

To our younger generation, I want to say: be proud of your country because it is the best in the world. Love your parents, guardians, and teachers — they are the foundation of your future. Stay away from booze, tobacco and drugs — they will tear you down. Be a good person at all times — you will never regret it. Try your best at all times — and you will have done your duty.

If this book helps someone to understand these things, and to remember and thank those who fought for freedom — not only in World War II, but in all the wars our country has fought — then I will have done my duty.

Addenda

My brothers

While I want this book to honor and remember all of the men and women who were in our country's military services in World War II, there are two men — **Frederick I. Dickerson** and **Herman E. Dickerson** — whose lives and service are especially meaningful to me, and one — **Glenn R. Dickerson** — who, although he couldn't serve in the military, was special, too.

My oldest and only surviving brother, Fred, was and is my hero. He is 87 years old now. He doesn't drink, smoke, or curse, and has always done his duty. He is a real gentleman and he has always been an inspiration to me.

Fred was born May 6, 1911. He graduated from Reidsville High School after playing football, basketball, baseball and track there. He was also one of the first Eagle Scouts in Rockingham County in 1926. He attended Elon College and then transferred to Lees-McRae Jr. College, where he played football, basketball, tennis and baseball.

After graduating from Lees-McRae, he went to Davidson College where he earned his BS degree while being a 4-letter athlete in football, basketball, baseball, and track, and winning the decathlon trophy. He also waited tables in the college cafeteria and served as president of his senior class while at Davidson. He went on to earn his MS degree from Louisiana State University before World War II.

During the war, Fred served in the Navy as

Fred, as he looked when he was coaching championship teams.

a Lieutenant Commander.

After the war and until his retirement, he had a distinguished career as a college coach and teacher, inspiring athletes at three different institutions — Mars Hill College, Davis and Elkins College, and Lees-McRae Jr. College.

Fred was a gentleman as an officer in the Navy during World War II, as a coach later, and continues to this day to be the finest man I know.

His athletic teams won 25 championships in football, basketball, and track.

Glenn was born August 19, 1913. As a young boy, he was a very good wood and soap carver. I remember that when Lindbergh flew the Atlantic, Glenn carved a plane that looked just like the *Spirit of St. Louis*. He put a rubber-band driven propeller on it and it would go along the floor just as pretty as you ever saw.

Glenn, as he looked in the 1950s. He was only 44 when he died of a heart attack.

Like Fred, Glenn attended Reidsville High School except that his last year of high school was at Greensboro High School, where he graduated. He then went to Lees-McRae Jr. College. He played football in high school and college, but wasn't as athletic as my other brothers, perhaps because at some point he had contracted tuberculosis (TB).

As a young man, he spent several years in a sanitarium because of his TB and that was where he learned the watchmaking and repairing trade. After being released from the sanitarium, he eventually opened up his own jewelry store in Dallas, Texas.

When the war broke out, Glenn couldn't join up because of his TB. He was still running his shop in Texas when he died of a heart attack on January 1, 1957.

Herman was born November 1, 1915. Following in our older brothers' footsteps, he attended Reidsville High School and graduated there, after playing baseball, basketball, track and football. He led his team to the state football championship in its division three times (1930, '31, and '32), while being named to the All-State football team twice (1932 and '33). Herman then went to VPI (Virginia Tech) where he earned honors as a first-team All-Southern and first-team *Sports Illustrated* All-American football player in 1936. His football exploits earned him a place on a professional football team — the Chicago Cardinals (later the St. Louis Cardinals) — in 1937

Herman cut a dashing figure as an officer in the paratroopers in WWII, and looked dignified and distinguished in his later years.

and the nickname, "Foots."

During the war, Herman entered the Army as a second lieutenant in the paratroopers, was promoted to captain, then major, and served in Europe as a battalion executive officer.

After the war, he had a number of positions in private companies before beginning his career in government as a city clerk and treasurer for St. Pauls, NC. He then served as city manager for Laurinburg, NC, assistant city manager for Charlotte, NC, and as city manager for Statesville, NC. He served the latter city for 24 years until his retirement in 1979. Herman died April 2, 1987.

Some of the mementos that I displayed in the den in our home at 1128 W. Northwood St., Greensboro. On the wall are photos of the three men I admire most: my brother, Fred Dickerson; my coach, Bob Jamieson; my commander, Lt. Gen. James Gavin.

Medals, badges and commendations awarded to Douglas Dickerson

Bronze Star with cluster

Purple Heart with cluster

Meritorious Service

Good Conduct

American Defense

Europe/Africa/Mid-East

Victory

Presidential Unit Citation with cluster

Meritorious Unit Citation

French Fourragere

Belgium Fourragere

Netherlands Lanyard

Combat Infantry Badge

Combat Wings

French Jubilee of Liberty Medal